WHAT CEO'S SAY ABOUT THE BOOK AND ITS CONCEPTS

"You told me to trust the process and 'it' would happen. Boy, were you right! Today, there's a different feel at QVC. The QVC Difference is making a difference in who we are as a company and what we are able to achieve. It's helping us every day in how we do things."

Doug Briggs,
Former CEO, QVC, Inc.

"In order to be a true global competitor, we realized it was critical to shift aspects of our culture. Senn-Delaney Leadership was invaluable in the development and implementation of this transformation process."

Ivan Seidenberg
Chairman and CEO, Verizon

"Your processes to bring the team together to create solid working relationships is the most effective I have encountered. They have not only helped us to focus on issues at work, but have added benefit in our personal lives outside the workplace. They provided the leadership necessary to address the competition, which we are reminded is outside—not inside—TVA."

Craven Crowell
Former Chairman, Tennessee Valley Authority (TVA)

"When I became chairman and CEO at Tenneco Automotive, I recognized that creating a high-performance organization would be critical to achieving long-term success. The Senn-Delaney processes have been invaluable in helping me make that happen."

Mark Frissora
Former Chairman, President and CEO, Tenneco

WHAT CEO'S SAY ABOUT THE BOOK AND ITS CONCEPTS

*"When I came in as the new CEO of Nationwide, I knew we need-
ed to shift some elements in the existing corporate culture. Senn-
Delaney Leadership has been our guide and coach on that journey.
Their processes, outlined in this book, have been instrumental to
these changes. They have helped me create a great team at the top
and helped create the culture which has supported improved bottom-line results."*

Jerry Jurgensen
Chairman and CEO, Nationwide

*"The concepts in the book are proving to be of great benefit to me
as a leader in building a great team and a healthy, high-performance culture."*

Larry Glasscock
Chairman, President and CEO, WellPoint, Inc.

*"The Senn-Delaney Leadership processes and concepts were
invaluable. They brought out the best in people and improved customer service, sales and bottom-line results."*

David Novak
Chairman, President and CEO, Yum! Brands, Inc.

*"We were able to enhance our effectiveness as individual leaders
and in so doing become a more effective senior leadership team.
Senn Delaney Leadership aided us in better aligning around our
vision, mission and values."*

Stein Kruse
President and CEO, Holland America Line, Inc.

Winning Teams

Winning Cultures

Larry E. Senn

Jim Hart

Foreword by Warren Bennis

lp

Leadership Press

A Leadership Press book, published by arrangement with the authors.

Library of Congress Control Number: 2006925063

Senn, Larry

Hart, Jim

Winning Teams—Winning Cultures

Includes index and sources.

1. Corporate Culture. 2. Culture Change. 3. Culture Clash.
4. Change Initiatives. 5. Change Management. 6. High-Performance
Culture,Teams. 6.Teambuilding. I. Senn, Larry E. II. Hart, Jim.
III. Title. IV. Title: Winning Teams—Winning Cultures

ISBN 0963601822 (hardcover)
ISBN 0963601849 (paperback)

First edition, September 2006

Printed in Korea by bigger dot

Printing number
1 2 3 4 5 6 7 8 9 0

Copies of *Winning Teams—Winning Cultures* are available at special discounts for
bulk purchases by corporations, institutions and other organizations.

For more information, please call, fax or write to:

The Leadership Press, Inc.
3780 Kilroy Airport Way, Suite 800
Long Beach, CA 90806
(800) 788-3380 Phone
(562) 426-5174 Fax

FOREWORD

〰

Foreword
by
Warren Bennis

Collaborative genius.

Today, most books and articles written on organizational change acknowledge the power of culture. We often see cultural issues at the heart of merger clashes, strategy failures or change initiatives. Unfortunately, culture is much like the weather—everyone talks about it with the assumption that nothing can be done about it. We thrive when the sun shines and take cover when winter winds blow. Fortunately, organizational culture is not quite so capricious. We are capable of charting a course through rain, sleet, snow and fair weather if we can maintain our sense of direction, understanding the values and behaviors that lie at the core of our organizations. Winning Teams– Winning Cultures provides an excellent guidance system for navigating these evolving cultural landscapes. The book's ideas, tools and techniques can turn any team you lead or any culture you are a part of, large or small, into one that is healthy and high-performing.

In today's complex workplace, a leader's success is directly related to the effectiveness of his teams. These teams make up the culture of the organization, and their health is a reflection of that culture's health. To realize the high-performance results we are after, we have to understand the power of these essential and healthy collaborations.

In *Co-Leaders*, a book I co-authored with David Heenan, we make the point that the genius of our age is truly collaborative. Because of the complexity of the issues we face, we need teams of leaders working toward a common purpose. We no longer live in a world in which individual stars can carry the day on their own. To truly succeed, we need high-performance teams and winning cultures. Winning Teams– Winning Cultures provides insight into the role corporate culture plays in all change initiatives. It offers practical ideas that can be successfully implemented and will allow you, your team and your organization to produce better results while, at the same time, supplying the personal fulfillment necessary for cultures to prosper.

My colleagues and I at the University of Southern California Marshall School of Business have been immersed in the study of leadership for many years. During that same period the authors and their teammates at Senn-Delaney Leadership have been working with and studying the impact of culture on organizational effectiveness. Long before the word "culture" appeared in a business journal, Larry Senn became intrigued with the personality of organizations. It was 35 years ago as a doctoral student here at USC that he completed the first systematic study of corporate culture and its impact on the results of organizations. Over the past 25 years, he and his organization have worked on the cultural aspects of mergers and acquisitions, on shifting cultures for deregulation, on privatization in Europe, and on the fast-paced Silicon Valley cultures. No one has had more experience in identifying the secret of a winning culture than the authors of this book.

Warren Bennis

Warren Bennis is the founding chairman of the Leadership Institute, University of Southern California; a distinguished professor of business administration at the University of Southern California; author of dozens of books including the classic best seller Leaders; *and consultant to hundreds of CEO's and four U.S. Presidents.*

TABLE OF CHAPTERS

INTRODUCTION

If you are a professional, then chances are you have an interest in the areas of leadership effectiveness, team effectiveness, and/or overall organizational culture. This book shares "a view from the field." It was written to capture many of the lessons Senn-Delaney Leadership has learned—after decades of work with hundreds of companies and thousands of leaders—about what is different in healthy, high-performance individuals, winning teams and winning cultures.

This book helps explain why two companies in the same industry, with similar strategies, equipment and pricing, (like Southwest Airlines and Delta's Song) achieve such different results. Or why a team made up of highly competent, knowledgeable and committed leaders can still be ineffective. Or why one leader can rise to the top of an organization, when another who is just as intelligent, well-educated and ambitious, is stalled many levels down.

Three Levels: Leaders, Teams and Cultures

We chose the title *Winning Teams—Winning Cultures* because we have found that organizations with long-term success have winning cultures—and those cultures are made up of leaders and teams with a definable set of winning behaviors. The three levels—the individual, the team and the culture—are interconnected. Our purpose in writing this book is to provide you with valuable knowledge at all three levels.

For You as an Individual

The ideas we cover in the following chapters can help you personally, not only with leadership effectiveness, but with overall life effectiveness. We explain how to:

- Create greater results with less time and effort
- Achieve more success with less stress

- Be an effective team leader and change agent

- Shape the "culture" of the team, unit or organization you lead

- Have more fulfilling relationships at work *and* at home

- Enjoy an even higher quality of life

For Your Team

Most of our time at work, and at home for that matter, is spent as part of a group of people—a team. One theme we focus on in this book is *winning teams*. You are probably a part of multiple teams: the team you lead, as well as all the teams to which you belong. And at some point in your life you have likely been a part of a team that really gelled. There were definable qualities that existed on that healthy, winning team. Chapter 4 talks about eight characteristics of a high-performance team. Those ideas can help you better contribute to a healthy, high-performing team of your own.

Shaping the Culture

> *"Every organization has a definable culture; the only question is, does it shape you or do you shape it?"*

Creating a winning organizational culture should be one of the highest priorities of any leader who wants long-term business success and an engaged, fulfilled workforce. That's why the third theme, building a winning culture, is the ultimate goal of this book as well as the vision and mission of Senn-Delaney Leadership: *to enhance the spirit and performance of organizations by creating healthy, high-performance cultures.*

The three levels of culture shaping—the individual, the team and the organization—are interconnected. You really can't change a culture without shifting the behaviors of individuals in that culture, and winning cultures are made up of collaborative, high-performance teams across the organization.

A Foundational Premise

There are moments when all individuals and teams are at their best and at the top of their game. This is akin to an athlete or a sports team when they are "in the zone." The difference is that being at your best is accessible to you much more often than those rare moments when an athlete is "in the zone." When we are at our best, we are accountable, collaborative, resourceful, optimistic, creative, agile and effective. We are less stressed, less worried, achieve greater results and get more fulfillment in life. We also are more likely to be connected to a higher goal such as making a difference or serving others, rather than being self-absorbed.

We believe that the qualities we have when we are at our best are part of our natural state of being. "Innate health" is contained within all of us, as are the resulting "default" life-effectiveness values. Unfortunately, over time we develop habits and thought systems, including win/lose beliefs, that override our natural state of healthy high-performance behaviors.

Senn-Delaney Leadership's work with individuals, teams and cultures is designed to re-anchor people more firmly to the best of who they already are. Rather than teaching dozens of techniques, our goal—in this book and in the work we do—is to connect you, your team and your organization to your innate values while providing pointers on how to stay at your best more of the time.

In Chapter 2 we offer a series of useful pointers for living life at your best. Chapter 4 describes the characteristics of a winning team, while Chapter 5 outlines a proven change model to help shape the culture of your organization or business unit.

The Origin of the Senn-Delaney Leadership Model

The ideas in this book were developed practically, not theoretically, from more than 40 years of hands-on work with organizations.

It all began in the early 1960s when Larry Senn accepted a teaching fellowship in the doctoral program of the University of Southern California's graduate school of business. At the same time, Larry joined his former industrial engineering professor from the University of California, Los Angeles, to help him with an overflow of outside consulting assignments. As the work grew, the professor needed more help and Jim Delaney, another of the professor's former students, joined them. After a few years, Senn and Delaney founded an operational consulting firm to improve the performance of organizations.

They quickly discovered three things:

1. It was easier to develop a plan for change than to get the people to change.

2. Every organization has a distinct and definable personality—and many were like dysfunctional families.

3. Characteristics in the invisible, or behavioral, side of the organization largely determined whether change initiatives succeeded or failed.

Larry labeled this phenomenon *organizational character* (a prelude to organizational culture). His conclusion was that the change initiatives they were asked to implement would not be consistently successful unless a way was found to overcome dysfunctional organizational habits and create the high-performance behavior to support the changes.

This realization led Larry to select corporate culture as the topic of his doctoral dissertation[1], referred to in the foreword by Warren Bennis. The study focused on six clients in the same industry: three were quite successful and three were struggling, with one on the verge of going out of business. The purpose was to identify the characteristics that existed in the teams and organizations that were successful, compared to the habits in the organizations that ultimately failed.

That work began to reveal the success factors we now call the *Essential Value Set* (see Chapter 8), which includes qualities like personal accountability vs. blaming, teamwork vs. protecting turf, trust vs. assumed motives, and openness vs. resistance to change.

In many ways the outcome of the study, completed in 1970, was a precursor to Tom Peters' *In Search of Excellence*[2], which was published more than a decade later.

Since cultural change requires behavioral change in both leaders and teams, Senn devoted much of the 1970s to developing more powerful learning models and processes to change habits of leaders. These processes formed a methodology to shape the behaviors of teams, which was then piloted and used as a front-end intervention to change initiatives being implemented by the Senn-Delaney operational improvement firm.

The success in supporting large-scale change initiatives led Senn to form a new and different kind of consulting company, Senn-Delaney Leadership, in 1978. It was the first and only consulting firm with a specific and singular mission: to shape the overall cultures of organizations to better support business results. Delaney remained with the original process-improvement firm, which was eventually sold to one of the "Big 6" accounting firms, and Senn focused his efforts on building Senn-Delaney Leadership as a culture-shaping firm.

Senn-Delaney Leadership has worked with hundreds of organizations and thousands of teams around the world for more than 25 years. This work has included transforming cultures in the rapidly changing telecommunications industry, privatizing firms in Europe, creating service cultures for retailers, dealing with the cultural aspects of mergers and acquisitions, and assisting dozens of CEOs in fostering the necessary behaviors in their senior teams and organizational cultures to drive their strategies and implement major initiatives.

While many people have contributed to the model and ideas expressed within these pages, two of the principal contributors are the co-authors of this book: Larry Senn, who pioneered the process and created the core change methodology, and Jim Hart, the current CEO of Senn-Delaney Leadership, who helped enhance the latest model for culture shaping. Another early contributor was John Childress, a previous Senn-Delaney Leadership CEO and co-author of a forerunner of this book, *The Secret of a Winning Culture*[3].

Whether you are a leader of a team, department, division or a Global 1000 firm, or a Human Resources professional tasked with developing leaders, teams or cultures, the principles and processes outlined here can help you and your team create the behaviors needed to better support your goals for long-term success.

Throughout this book, Larry Senn and Jim Hart will provide personal examples of various concepts, written in first person. We will note this by prefacing the text with their first names (i.e., "Larry:" or "Jim:").

1

THE JAWS OF CULTURE

WHY IS CULTURE SHAPING AN IMPERATIVE FOR ANY LEADER?

If you are not sure why culture is important, just consider these questions:

- What is it that makes implementing any change harder?

- What is the biggest contributor to lack of full employee engagement?

- Why do major systems installations cost more, take longer and deliver less than expected?

- What is the number one reason customers aren't treated well?

- Why don't reorganizations solve turf issues?

- What is the main reason for the failure of mergers and acquisitions?

Answer: *It's the culture.*

Anyone who has ever tried to implement change quickly learns that the shortfall in results is rarely due to purely technical or operational issues. It is almost always the result of human issues.

That was our experience when Senn-Delaney originally started out as a process improvement firm. When implementation felt like pulling a car with flat tires up a hill, it was because of dysfunctional organizational habits. In contrast, when results came faster and easier, healthy high-performance behaviors were alive in the culture.

This discovery seemed to have a direct parallel to life itself. Most of the reasons people fail in jobs and come up short in their careers are due to personality and behavioral issues, not job knowledge or technical competence.

well-intioned
but
dysfx habits

As we worked to improve the performance of clients, we soon learned another important lesson:

It is easier to decide on change than to get people to change!

People and organizations are creatures of habit, and changing habits is much harder than changing structures or systems. It seemed to us that teams and organizations, like people, had personalities; and to ignore or not deal with an organization's personality traits could be fatal to our change efforts.

We call this phenomenon the *jaws of culture* because cultural habits, such as resistance to change and turf issues, chew up the improvement process and reduce or eliminate the results (Figure 1.1).

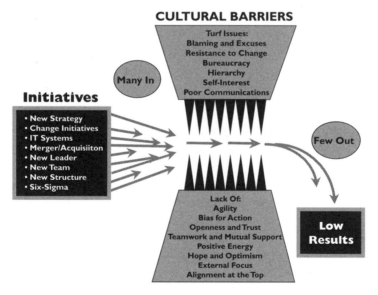

Figure 1.1 © 2006 Senn-Delaney Leadership Consulting Group, LLC.

"Corporate culture—those hard to change values that spell success and failure."

—*Business Week*[4]

We believe that the "jaws" are the reason that most initiatives and strategies fall short of their potential. Well-intentioned but dysfunctional habits in your culture or team can literally stop your change effort dead in its tracks.

As we witnessed change efforts falter time after time, we began to say to one another privately, and with some amusement, "It's the culture, dummy!"

Be aware of the jaws of culture. The sharp, shark-like teeth can quickly kill your change initiatives.

The jaws of culture destroy change initiatives in a variety of ways. The following classic examples, as related to us by senior executives, are all too familiar:

"The numbers showed the merger/acquisition would really pay off, but we're losing some of the best talent in the acquired firm, we've lost some key customers, and we are running into more conflict than we expected. It's a real clash of cultures."

"The restructure was supposed to break down the barriers between divisions and create a more collaborative organization. Instead, we just created new turf issues. It must be in the genes."

"The latest strategy sounded great, but we haven't been able to execute it with our slow-moving, risk-averse, bureaucratic culture."

"The new I.T. system should have been up and running last quarter, saving us time and money. There is a lot of finger-pointing going on now because it's behind schedule and won't deliver all we thought it would."

"The analysis showed we would see dramatic savings through process improvement, but so far we haven't had many savings. Where are all the results? And why is everyone so upset?"

"We just completed another record quarter, and I should be feeling great. The fact is I'm not. I'm paying too big a price personally trying to make things happen in this culture and I don't know if it's worth it to stay in this game."

Change initiatives fail more often than they succeed. In one survey cited in *Harvard Business Review*, 75 percent of managers polled were unhappy with change initiatives underway.[5] Most people don't need a lot of data; they know through experience, or intuitively, when a change is not going as planned. The reality is:

> **The success of any change is tied to human dynamics (the culture).**

And yet, most change initiatives continue to focus almost exclusively on the operational, systems and technical side. What they too often ignore, or at best give lip service to, is the human or behavioral side of change.

Fortunately, most leaders today recognize, at least intellectually, that culture plays a role in results. The business world is slowly beginning to appreciate the power of cultural habits. Most change initiatives have token elements of "change management," but these rarely address culture. They are mostly communications plans that *inform* but do not *transform*. Most organizations still don't address culture barriers as vigorously or systematically as they should.

The only way to ensure the maximum success of any broad-based change initiative is to systematically deal with the culture.

Successful business transformation requires true cultural transformation.

If you have ever tried to make changes or implement improvement initiatives in an unreceptive culture, you know it is like trying to swim against the current. You put in a lot of effort but don't make much forward progress.

Organizations can benefit from restructuring, business transformation efforts, Six Sigma, process improvements, Customer Relationship Management (CRM), and customer service initiatives but in most cases the efforts will fall far short of full potential. It's not that the process isn't appropriate; it's that it is applied in a culture where the new approaches can't fully "take."

The importance of aligning strategy and culture was stated well in a *Business Week* article:

"A corporation's culture can be its greatest strength when it is consistent with its strategies. But a culture that prevents a company from meeting competitive threats, or from adapting to changing economic or social environments, can lead to the company's stagnation and ultimate demise."

—*Business Week*[6]

When an organization's cultural barriers are well understood and addressed, a much higher percentage of change efforts achieve their full potential.

CULTURAL BARRIERS

We have identified ten of the most common cultural barriers. Which ones, if any, exist in your organization?

1. Internal competition between business units and functions—turf issues and "we-they" attitudes

2. Lack of agility or ability to quickly adapt

3. Hierarchical top-down tendencies and a boss-driven leadership style

4. Bureaucratic tendencies and lack of innovation

5. An "observer-critic" culture that kills new ideas

6. Entitlement mindset and poor empowerment

7. Lack of accountability, excessive blaming and excuses—"not my fault"

8. Trust issues and hidden agendas

9. Inability to foster and support diversity of ideas and people

10. Conflict avoidance and polite, but passive-aggressive, behaviors

All change initiatives must pass through these and other teeth in the jaws of culture. Most get chewed up before they ever accomplish their full objectives. While every company and team is different, each has its own barriers that comprise the "jaws" of culture. What are yours?

Sometimes cultural barriers can be more easily recognized in the context of specific business issues or events. Here are some common business situations where the jaws of culture can show their teeth.

MERGERS/ACQUISITIONS AND CULTURAL CLASH   *what would acquisitions look like in academia?*

The most widely recognized cultural challenge is in the area of mergers and acquisitions. Few business journals talk about mergers without exploring the potential for "cultural clash." Learning how to avoid cultural clash is important to a leader because acquisitions will always be a part of the strategy of most growing companies. Acquisitions are important because of:

- A need for greater size or scale to better compete

- A need for broader competitive skills through alliances and acquisitions

- A need to create broader geographic presence or coverage

- A need to grow beyond the rate of organic growth alone

- Continuing consolidation in many industries

The reality is most mergers and acquisitions fall short of potential and many fail. The most common reason for this is cultural clash.

"When companies combine, a clash of cultures can turn potentially good business alliances into financial disasters."

—Psychology Today, "The Merger Syndrome"[7]

While it is clear that a merger or acquisition must be based on solid financial data and other objective elements, like geographic and strategic fit, ignoring the corporate culture can be a recipe for disaster. Far too often, differences in management styles and cultures are not considered during the pre-acquisition process. As a result, many acquisitions that looked very promising from a strategic or financial viewpoint in the pre-merger phase fall apart in the implementation phase.

"When the deal is inked and the financial wizards go home, that's when the trouble starts. You've got the numbers. Now, what are you going to do about the people?"

—Training Magazine, *"The Forgotten Factor in Merger Mania"*[8]

Well-known examples of the impact of culture on the success of mergers and acquisitions can be found regularly in business journals and newspapers. They include Compaq and Digital, AOL Time Warner and Disney's acquisition of Fox Family.

Cultural incompatibility is the largest cause of 1) poor merger performance; 2) departure of key executives; and 3) time-consuming conflicts when trying to integrate organizations.

The Bureau of Business Research at American International College conducted a survey in which the CFO and other key financial executives from 45 Fortune 500 firms (with sales totaling over $240 billion) said that incompatibility of the corporate cultures, much more than financial or planning mistakes, is the most likely and damaging factor that prevents mergers and alliances from achieving their desired synergy and full potential.[9]

Think of a merger as a marriage. Two companies merging based on financial data alone would be like two people marrying based solely on height, weight and vital statistics—both lead to divorce.

The key to avoiding disaster is to deal more systematically with the cultural aspect of the merger. A cultural assessment and integration strategy can overcome cultural clash.

One example of this is the acquisition of several hundred Safeway stores in Southern California by Vons several years ago. The leader of Vons sensed there were differences that might get in the way. Safeway had survived in Southern California with an entrepreneurial, customer-focused neighborhood strategy. The store managers selected goods that fit each locale, paid a lot of attention to the checkout lines, and provided friendly service to customers and a cordial working environment for employees. That was the good news. The bad news was that they tended to neglect the appearance of the store, orderliness of the shelves and dating on merchandise. They also paid less attention to labor costs and details of the stores' revenue.

Vons was the exact opposite. They were very centrally managed with strong financial controls. Store managers knew the revenue numbers. They closely managed labor costs and each store was very orderly, clean and always up-to-date. Vons was more profit-driven and disciplined. At the same time, they were less employee and customer-friendly. Managers were bosses more than coaches.

In a process we conducted to sensitize the Vons field managers to Safeway, we asked the Vons district managers who supervised stores, "What would you do if you went into a Vons store and it looked like a Safeway store does now, and was off a bit on its numbers?" One guy yelled out, "We'd be kicking ass and taking names!" He quickly added, "Oh, we'd probably lose all the Safeway store managers, wouldn't we?" That was a significant "Ah-ha!" moment because they all had been told that the key to the acquisition's success was the retention of those hard-to-find-and-train store managers.

The Vons District managers went on to talk about a more sensitive way to gradually achieve the relationship they wanted with Safeway, through a coaching process vs. as drill sergeants. They also acknowledged that there were several things Safeway did very well that they could learn from.

With some training and coaching, the acquisition turned out well and few Safeway store managers were lost. In an ironic footnote to the story, a few years later the Safeway parent organization purchased Vons and owns them today.

Culture and the New Leader

Have you ever wondered why a CEO or other leader who is very successful at one firm has a hard time getting on track when moving to a new firm? In more cases than not, he or she has not figured out or been able to overcome the new culture. A recent study showed that 40 percent of new chief executives fail within 18 months.[10]

New leaders have what we call "stranger's eyes." As they come into an organization, most of the cultural problems are very apparent to them, yet they may be invisible to people who have been there for years. The new leader often has a sense of urgency about making change and starts to take on some of the culture's "sacred cows" in terms of both customs and people. Since organizations, like all organisms, fight to maintain the status quo, sometimes the leader wins and sometimes the culture wins. Most commonly, the change comes far slower than the leader would like, which can lead to years of frustration on both the part of the leader and the people within the organization.

The question soon becomes:

"Will the culture get them, or will they get the culture?"

We once worked with a very successful and talented CEO. His success made him a target of recruiters and boards seeking to fill CEO slots. He was recruited to help "fix" a large underperforming railroad. He came in as a proven general manager but he was not a "railroad guy." Unfortunately for him, the railroad industry has a very deeply ingrained culture and a history of rejecting non-railroad people. The industry is, in general, very traditional, resistant to change with long-tenured managers and, as might be expected, has a strong "old boy" network. The new CEO easily saw much of what needed to be done and set about to do it. All efforts fell short and he was gone in 18 months. The culture won and the company lost, because they didn't have a plan and proven process to change the culture.

Jack Welch talked with us about the phenomenon he faced when he took over as CEO of General Electric (GE). He had successfully run a smaller, more agile plastics division, where he found it was relatively easy to formulate and execute plans successfully. Welch told us he got his reputation for being a very hard-edged leader while trying to overcome the old GE culture.

> *"I realized the bureaucracy ran things and the resistance to change was incredible, and that I had to shed tons of layers, a lot of bureaucracy and all the form-over-substance behavior that exists in a big company. In doing so I became known as 'Neutron Jack.' But I had to deal with an organization that had become a huge bureaucracy."*[11]

Welch also acknowledged that he tried initially to muscle through the culture and was not successful. That experience caused him to set up the John F. Welch Leadership Center at Crotonville (located in Ossining, New York) and introduce the GE Values as a way to more proactively shape the culture to support his business strategies. As he put it, *"Values are a key to success at GE. We spend a lot of time talking about what values a leader has to have."*[12]

In the case of GE, Welch changed the culture; it didn't "get" him.

Jaws of Culture vs. IT Systems and Business Process Improvement

With the best intentions, hundreds of companies each year embark on major organization-wide systems and process improvement initiatives. Some succeed in spite of the culture, but many fall short because of it. A study conducted by Arthur D. Little, Inc., reported that only 16% of 350 executives interviewed said they were fully satisfied with the results of their change efforts. In fact, 68% of these executives reported that their change initiatives created additional problems that were unintended at the beginning of the process.[13]

We Know It—Why Don't We Deal With It?

For anyone who has ever been through a performance improvement effort, it doesn't take studies to prove that "people issues" are the greatest barriers to success. So if we know it, why don't we deal with it?

Unfortunately, corporate leaders all too often underestimate the difficulty of implementing a major shift in processes, systems or structure. The shift from the old ways of doing things to new ways leaves every person involved in a state of uncertainty and confusion. Will the new ways work? What will my role be? Can I handle the new work? Will I have a new boss who will treat me fairly? Will I like my new co-workers? Will I still have my place in the new scheme of things?

In an interview we had with Jack Welch in 1993, he summarized his thoughts on the difficulty of implementing a major change initiative and what is required for success:

> *"When I try to summarize what I've learned, one of the big lessons is that change has no constituency. People like the status quo. They like the way it was. When you start changing things, the good old days look better and better."*[14]

Strategy Implementation and Culture

Leaders become very aware of the need to change their culture when new strategies are not working as planned. Here are some examples of disconnects:

- They want to be more externally customer-focused, but cannot overcome their internal operational focus.

- They need to implement more effective, cross-functional shared services but are siloed—and not collaborative.

- They want to grow through acquisitions, but acquisitions aren't paying off because they keep encountering cultural clashes.

- They need to implement organization-wide CRM, SAP (systems applications and products in data processing) or ERP (enterprise resource planning systems) but business units resist sharing systems.

Most companies have cultures that work reasonably well for past strategies. New strategies almost always require a shift in some elements of the culture. Specific strategies need specific cultural strengths to work best. Here are a few examples:

Need for a collaborative culture

Teamwork, trust and high levels of collaboration are needed for:

- Movement from a holding company to an allied or shared business model

- Implementation of shared services

- Cross selling and "solution vs. product" sales strategies

- Matrixed or project-based organizations

One example of collaborative culture is the need to present one face to the customer. This need can exist for a bank, computer company or defense contractor. To present a "solution," not a product, different parts of their organization need to work together unselfishly to provide the type of integrated offering today's customers demand. Non-collaboration can become a huge cultural barrier. The strategy of "one face with an integrated solution" fails too often because many organizations are still a collection of autonomous power-bases making decisions in self-interest rather than for the greater organizational good.

Need for a recognition-based, positive and supportive culture

A positive, optimistic environment with high levels of trust and appreciation, as well as, employee and customer recognition and respect is needed to:

- Become a great place to work and an employer of choice

- Provide exceptional customer service

- Retain talent and reduce turnover

- Stimulate full engagement of employees

As an example, retailers who want improved customer service need to treat employees better. You can't get one without the other. That was the reason David Novak, current Chairman, CEO and President of Yum! Brands focused on a recognition culture when he first took over as CEO at KFC and later of Yum! Brands overall.

Our research with fast-food store teams confirms that service, sales and employee engagement improve when store teams feel valued, recognized and aligned in their commitment to the customer.

A department store group we worked with coined the phrase "Great Place to Work – Great Place to Shop" in recognition of the fact that the two were just different sides of the same coin.

Need for Agility

Openness, agility, resilience and decisions for the greater good are needed to implement:

- Major structural or systems changes

- Quick adjustments to changing industry or market conditions

- An initiative to become more innovative

Boeing/IDS faced this challenge after the consolidation of four major defense companies. They needed to change their organizational model from individual legacy companies to a more integrated and competitive single enterprise. They also needed to become much more agile and innovative to convert from operating within individual silos to being a competitive, integrated, network-centric firm. By moving toward this kind of culture, they were better able to sell and deliver on billions of dollars in new defense contracts which required an integrated systems approach.

Need for Personal Accountability

Extremely high levels of personal accountability to do the right thing, and a willingness to speak up and challenge authority, are needed when:

- Safety is paramount

- Reliability is a life-and-death matter

- Quality is essential to market success

Accountability vs. blaming shows up in a very special way in situations where safety and reliability are important. Two historic and disastrous events come to mind. The first is the near melt-down of the Three Mile Island Nuclear Plant, and the second is the Challenger shuttle disaster. In both cases the culture was the culprit. More specifically, post-mortems of these two events revealed that although some people on the team, usually below top management, knew something was wrong, the issues were never addressed.

In the case of the Challenger disaster, the potential issue of the O-ring had been discussed by lower level teams and some even felt strongly enough about it that they recommended against the launch. In both cases, there were hierarchical cultures where lower levels didn't feel empowered to raise these critical issues to senior leaders. Because the culture was one that lacked personal accountability, those that knew of the problems weren't persistent enough or willing to take the necessary risks to keep the issue on the table.

Senn-Delaney Leadership worked on the restart of Three Mile Island to help overcome the cultural issues at the core of the infamous incident. After our cause-and-effect diagnostics, we developed a core values-based leadership training program for all managers and control room operators. The foundation was personal accountability and the willingness to speak up. The theme: "If safety is to be, it's up to me."

The Tennessee Valley Authority, on the other hand, demonstrates the benefits of a strong and healthy culture. They spent years working on their Star 7 values-based culture, which included elements such as individual accountability and integrity. As a result, they have consistently operated some of the most reliable and safe nuclear power plants in the world. All are ranked INPO 1 (top 1% global) by the Institute of Nuclear Power Operations.

THE CULTURE AND INTEGRITY

There is more focus now on the ethical practices of leaders in business than ever before. The intense drive to improve quarterly earnings, especially during the tech bubble of the late 1990's and early 2000's, brought to light some ethical dysfunctions in organizations. The extreme pressure on performance, together with a lack of ethics, integrity and accountability, all contributed to those financial disasters. Those organization's leaders *did* know what was going on. They didn't do enough to confront it.

A *Los Angeles Times* article carried the headline, "Enron Schemes Reflect Culture." William Powers Jr., currently the president of the University of Texas at Austin, wrote the *Report Of Investigation By The Special Investigative Committee Of The Board Of Directors Of Enron Corp.*, analyzing Enron's failure. He said, "This is a cultural issue as much as an accounting issue. This is a matter of corporate character and virtue."[15] Enron's culture was a direct reflection of their leadership.

Failures like this illustrate the incredible power of a company's culture. High levels of personal accountability to speak up combined with ethics and integrity are needed to avoid issues symbolized by Enron. It is often invisible to us, so we aren't always fully aware of what we are up against. Recognizing it is the first step in addressing it.

ACTION STEPS: EXERCISE IN CULTURAL AWARENESS

Assessing your own culture

To better understand the strengths and challenges in the culture of your firm, business unit, department, function or team, take a moment to fill out the Corporate Culture Profile™ (CCP) below, which measures 23 cultural dimensions (Figure 1.2). If you look at the highest scores and the lowest scores, you will probably notice a pattern. (The CCP™ and its use is described in more detail in Chapter 6 on Diagnosis and Chapter 15 on Measurement.)

C VM

Top 3 Strengths	Strengths	Always	Mostly	Occasionally	Sometimes Both	Occasionally	Mostly	Always	Challenges	Top 3 Challenges
	Describe Your Perception of Your Company									
1	People clearly understand vision, mission and goals.	7	6	5	4	3	2	1	People are unclear about vision, mission and goals.	1
2	Clear alignment/common focus of leadership at top.	7	6	5	4	3	2	1	Obvious lack of alignment at the top.	2
3	Two-way frequent open communications.	7	6	5	4	3	2	1	Top-down, inadequate communications.	3
4	Flexible/fluid/empowered.	7	6	5	4	3	2	1	Hierarchical/boss driven.	4
5	High quality awareness and focus.	7	6	5	4	3	2	1	Quality not a high priority.	5
6	High service consciousness/focus on customer.	7	6	5	4	3	2	1	Low service consciousness/lack of focus on the customer.	6
7	Teamwork/mutual support and cooperation.	7	6	5	4	3	2	1	Narrow focus/turf issues/we versus they.	7
8	High performance expectations.	7	6	5	4	3	2	1	Low performance expectations.	8
9	Self starters/high initiative.	7	6	5	4	3	2	1	Need direction/low initiative.	9
10	Sense of urgency/bias for action.	7	6	5	4	3	2	1	Indecisive/bureaucratic/slow to respond.	10
11	People are highly accountable for results and actions.	7	6	5	4	3	2	1	People find excuses/blame others/feel victimized.	11
12	Open to change.	7	6	5	4	3	2	1	Resistant to change.	12
13	Encouraged to innovate/creativity welcomed.	7	6	5	4	3	2	1	Do what is told/risk averse/poor support for new ideas.	13
14	High levels of feedback and coaching.	7	6	5	4	3	2	1	Infrequent or no feedback and coaching.	14
15	High performance is recognized and rewarded.	7	6	5	4	3	2	1	High performance is expected but not recognized or rewarded.	15
16	Core values and ethics are very important.	7	6	5	4	3	2	1	Values and ethics not stressed or tend to be ignored.	16
17	People feel appreciated and valued.	7	6	5	4	3	2	1	People don't feel appreciated and valued.	17
18	High trust/openness between people.	7	6	5	4	3	2	1	Low trust/lack of openness.	18
19	Healthy/fast paced environment.	7	6	5	4	3	2	1	High stress/burnout pace.	19
20	Positive/optimistic/forgiving.	7	6	5	4	3	2	1	Insecure/fearful or negative environment.	20
21	Focused/balanced/effective.	7	6	5	4	3	2	1	Distracted/overwhelmed/inefficient.	21
22	Respect for diversity of ideas and people.	7	6	5	4	3	2	1	Lack of respect for diversity of ideas and people.	22

Figure 1.2 © 2006 Senn-Delaney Leadership Consulting Group, LLC.

Once you have completed the cultural profile, think of any goal you are trying to execute, or any strategy or initiative you are trying to achieve. Then ask yourself, "What are our jaws of culture? What three cultural barriers or habits are getting in the way or slowing down our progress toward the outcome?"

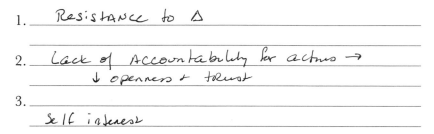

1. Resistance to Δ

2. Lack of Accountability for actions →
   ↓ openness + trust

3.
   Self interest

Now answer the question, "If I had a magic wand, what three qualities would I change in the organization to better support my outcomes?"

1. trust

2. valuing others + ideas, encouragement

3. no silos, no us vs them

This exercise, done thoughtfully, should give you a clue regarding the needs for culture shaping in your own organization or team.

Enlightened leaders see culture as an important lever in achieving business results. When they invest in it, the teeth in the "jaws of culture" are dulled and converted to cultural launching pads for greater organizational success.

2

PERSONAL TRANSFORMATION AS THE FOUNDATION OF CULTURAL TRANSFORMATION

You Can't Get Cultural Transformation Without Personal Transformation

One of Senn-Delaney Leadership's key premises in the work we do is that you can't build a winning culture without changing the behaviors of the individuals that make up that culture. Cultural transformation requires personal transformation.

The good news is that the behaviors needed in a healthy, high-performance culture are the same ones individuals need for a fulfilling life. A winning culture includes collaboration, personal responsibility, learning and growing, respect, trust and many other important personal values. Fortunately, it turns out that we don't need to learn these values—we already have them. They show up automatically when we are at our best. The trick is to be at our best more often.

At Your Best

When we ask groups to describe the behaviors they exhibit when they are at their best—what might be called at the "top of their game"—they can quickly create a list that includes feelings and behaviors like confidence, hopefulness, optimism, resourcefulness, collaboration, positive energy, creativity, inclusiveness, accountability and commitment. The list is not the way they think they *should* be; it's just the way they are when they are at their best. The list almost always encompasses what we call the "Essential Value Set." Our conclusion is that when people, teams and organizations are at their best, they naturally exhibit their own innate health in the form of essential values: the same kind of values required in a healthy culture.

Our work in recent years in strengthening the culture of our own firm has led us to conclude that organizational health emanates from the state of mind, or moods, of individuals within the organization. The Mood Elevator on the opposite page is a useful tool to gauge your state of mind and inner feelings at any moment in time. When you are higher on the Mood Elevator, you are at your best. When you are on the lower floors, chances are you aren't working effectively.

At Our Worst

Observing people and teams when they are at their worst provides the answer to where the dysfunctional behaviors in the "jaws of culture" come from. When we ask people to make a list of what they feel like when they are not at their best, the list includes words like worried, judgmental, territorial, victimized, threatened, impatient, angry and even depressed. Once again, this list is nothing more than the group's description of their lower floors of the Mood Elevator. Their description of how they behave when at their worst summarizes all the classic dysfunctions or cultural barriers that organizations face. This includes being less accountable, less collaborative, less trusting and less open to change or new ideas.

Understanding Where Moods Come From

Some days we are more hopeful and optimistic, and other days more worried. In some meetings we are judgmental and others, just curious. Our state of mind often takes the form of moods, which move from high to low, much like an elevator. While they are a part of the normal human condition, our moods have great implications. The trick is not to get off, move in and furnish any of the lower floors. Have you ever known someone who moved in on the impatient, irritated or judgmental floor?

Our thinking creates our state of mind as well as our experience of life.

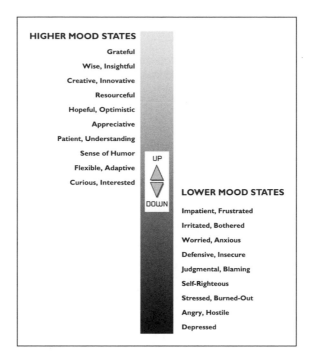

Figure 2.1 © 2006 Senn-Delaney Leadership Consulting Group, LLC.

The feelings on the Mood Elevator (Figure 2.1) are nothing more than products of our thinking. Worried thoughts create worried feelings, just as grateful thoughts produce grateful feelings. As an example, when we have worried thoughts, we have most of the same feelings as if the thing we're worried about actually happened. (And it usually doesn't.) This can have a profound impact on our quality of life. Just imagine how much better your experience of life would have been if you had simply not worried about the things that never happened.

The higher levels of the Mood Elevator are the result of what we call higher-level thinking. They are more clear, fresh, wise and resourceful. We are almost always *at our best* when we are operating there.

At the lower levels of the Mood Elevator we have lower quality thoughts. These thoughts are usually busier, less clear and often circular (worry goes around and around). It is usually less reliable although often compelling.

When we ask people what they "feel like" when they are at their best, the list looks surprisingly like the upper states of the Mood Elevator. They have a sense of humor, and feel more hopeful, optimistic, resourceful, patient, appreciative and grateful.

The overall conclusion is that when individuals, teams or organizations are operating "up the Mood Elevator," they are at their best as a leader, high-performance team or culture. An organization operating up the Mood Elevator has high levels of organizational health.

The benefits from operating in the higher states are enormous. A frenzied and stressed state of mind tends to decrease effectiveness. Daniel Goleman's books, *Emotional Intelligence*[16] and *Primal Leadership*[17], make an excellent case that we lose our wisdom and have a lower IQ when we are in a lower mood state. This can be seen in the unhealthy "bunker mentality" that exists in some companies going through change. When changes such as restructuring, mergers and acquisitions, and major system implementations are taking place in such a low mood state, more time is spent on rumors, speculation and avoiding change than on running the business.

When we are at the lower levels of the Mood Elevator, we often don't function as well at openness, teamwork, accountability, coaching, change or any of the other high-performance values or behaviors. In these lower mood states we are generally less creative; less able to inspire, motivate, and influence others; and less able to draw the line between our job and our life.

In the higher mood states, we tend to have more perspective. We are not gripped by the discussion, the issue or the project. A higher state of mind automatically gives added perspective and allows us to deal with difficult business problems in more creative and effective ways. The higher mood states enable us to:

- Listen more deeply

- Hear the hidden meanings

- Have more wisdom

- Focus on the big picture

- Influence others more effectively

- Worry less

- Keep our bearings despite the turmoil

- Have a better overall quality of life, both at work and at home

When a team and an organization can learn to operate in a healthier state, they can dramatically increase their performance. They can:

- Reach good decisions more easily and quickly

- Be more supportive internally and more competitive externally

- Align and positively energize the organization

- Handle whatever comes along, with greater grace and ease

We can be better team players, better coaches, more accountable, more open and accept change with greater ease when we are in higher states of mind.

Because we are human, we will visit most levels of the Mood Elevator at one time or another. We all will have days and moments when we are worried, bothered and impatient. It is a part of life to experience a full range of feelings. We shouldn't beat ourselves up or make ourselves feel wrong for visiting lower levels. That can just make it worse. We should recognize we are "off our game" and proceed with some caution until our natural healthier state returns. Unfortunately, some people not only ride the Mood Elevator, but get off and fully furnish the lower floors, including defensiveness, blame and judgment.

Moods play a big role in meetings. When a group tries to explore issues or make decisions while at the lower mood levels, it rarely works well. If you've ever wondered why a meeting was so draining and so few conclusions were reached, it probably was the state of mind of the group that day.

What is normal in your organization and your meetings? Is frustration, lack of trust, unhealthy conflict and high stress a way of life?

Even unhealthy states can become normal to us, and therefore invisible. It's like living alongside a freeway for a few months and no longer noticing the noise or the fumes. We can sometimes see our predicament if we have a quiet vacation and then step back into the storm at work. We now notice that the pace is frenetic and the noise is louder.

Since the health in an organization is a composite of each individual's mood state, here are some hints that can help minimize the adverse affects of lower moods and, in time, allow people to spend more time in the higher states, automatically helping the company move to a higher state of organizational health.

1. **Be conscious and aware of your mood state.** Post a copy of the Mood Elevator graphic where you can see it often, or just begin to notice the clues for when you drop to the lower states. Do you feel more impatient, more intense, more judgmental? Notice the clues that tell you when you are in the lower states.

2. **When on the lower levels of the Mood Elevator, remember that thoughts are usually unreliable.** There is a tendency to misinterpret events and actions and see others in a negative light when on these lower levels. A good night's sleep or added perspective will probably make things look different. Just recognizing that you are in a lower mood state gives the mood less power. If you can realize that this is just a temporary flurry of negative thoughts and not a permanent condition, then the thoughts have less power over you. When in the lower states, remind yourself to hold your thoughts lightly—don't grip them for dear life!

A useful metaphor is a horror movie. While watching an engaging, scary film, we can experience some fear. At the same time, at some level we know we are in a movie theater and it's only an illusion. Our momentary thoughts in lower states of mind about our job, our future or other people are rarely what they appear to be, much like a film.

3. **Be aware that in the lower states you are not as effective.** You don't do as well at things like collaboration, decision-making and problem-solving. Just being conscious of your state of mind can be useful. As a general rule, it is rarely a good idea to make a big decision in a lower mood state. Your judgment is impaired and your lenses to the world are clouded.

When you are feeling angry or judgmental, you can't do a good job at giving another person coaching and feedback. Have you ever tried to give a loved one feedback when you (or they) were in a lower state? If you had any success, you're very unusual.

Have you tried to collaborate on a team with someone when you both were resentful, untrusting or judgmental? Once again, it's a recipe for failure.

On the other hand, teaming, coaching and creative decision-making all come more easily and naturally in the higher states of mind.

4. **Learn to recognize your own "unhealthy normal."** Many people who live in Los Angeles stop recognizing the smog. People who live near an airport after a time don't notice the noise. Both situations could be called *unhealthy normal*. When it comes to mood states, we each have our own unhealthy normal. It is a mood state that occurs so frequently that we no longer notice it. Since the key to doing something about moods is noticing when you are there, it is important to move things out of that unhealthy normal category. What's your unhealthy normal? Is it being impatient, judgmental, worried or angry? Once a loud bell goes off each time you head for that state, you will be able to do something about it.

5. **Take better care of yourself.** There is a connection between our physical well-being and our state of mind. Have you ever had a really bad day, gotten a good night's sleep and found things look much better the next morning? Adequate rest, a healthy diet and regular exercise can go a long way toward giving us much more resilience in the area of our mood states.

6. **Don't be hard on yourself when you are on the lower floors**. Everyone spends some time there. Don't work too hard at getting up. Sometimes it just takes some time for a mood to pass, just like the weather. It *does* help to be aware it's your thinking and to know that it will pass and things will look better.

7. **Keep things in perspective.** When you are in a bad mood or low state, things that bother you can be all-consuming. You can become gripped by them. Generally, if you look at the bigger picture in your total life including your health, your loved ones, your other accomplishments, or your life beyond work, things can be put into better perspective.

There are two kinds of perspective that can be of particular help. The first is a "gratitude perspective." In short, this means count your blessings. Many high-achieving people focus almost solely on what isn't; that includes the goal they haven't reached, what they or someone else hasn't done perfectly. If you take a moment to look at what you have (health, job, loved ones), your spirits will be lifted and you will be more effective in your work and your life.

LARRY: I carry a picture in my wallet of my wife, 15-year-old daughter and 6-year old son, and another of a vacation spot on the beach in Hawaii. When I'm feeling a little low and it's late at night on the road or when I'm facing a particularly challenging situation, I take out the pictures to remind myself of my total life and what's really important. That tends to bring me perspective.

The second form of perspective is a "humor perspective." An expert on the benefits of humor in the workplace, C. W. Metcalf says, "Take yourself lightly and your job or problem seriously."[18] Humor automatically puts us in the higher mood states.

The higher mood states are lighter, more creative ones. If someone does something you believe is strange, you have a choice. You can go to the lower states and be irritated or angry, or you can go to the higher states and be interested or amused. The latter will give you a clearer head and better mental traction to deal with the situation.

8. **Use Your Feelings as Your Guide.** Sometimes when you are in a lower state of mind, your own "horror movies" seem totally real. The boss is a jerk, your teammate did cross you, your mate isn't understanding, and the world or your job is bleak. This inability to have perspective causes you to act when you shouldn't and say things you later regret.

There is an early warning system built into everyone. It is a way to know when our thinking is reliable and when we are viewing the world through a dark set of glasses: our feelings. Obvious indications of less reliable, lower-state thinking include:

- Reaction

- Negative intensity

- Anger

- Judgments and resentment

- Despair and hopelessness

Since we each have our own signals, learning to notice our feelings, moderate our behaviors and discount our lower states of thinking help us to be more effective leaders and have a better overall quality of life.

Higher mood state indicators also exist. They include positive feelings like:

- Hopefulness

- Optimism

- Gratitude

- A sense of well being

- Confidence that things can be handled and will work out

- In-the-moment perspective, such as, "My life is more than my job"

These feelings accompany our wisest thinking and are a more resourceful, creative and balanced approach to work and life.

MOOD STATES AND CULTURE

Individuals, teams and organizations all ride the Mood Elevator. The better the individuals and teams are at operating in the higher mood states and at their best, the easier it is to have a winning culture (Figure 2.2).

Healthy State of Mind/ Higher Mood State		**A Healthy Culture**
Gratitude Appreciation Curiosity Insight—Creativity Optimism—Hopefulness Sense of Humor	**Creates**	Teamwork Openness to Change Personal Accountability Mutual Respect Openness and Trust Caring About Customers Innovation

Figure 2.2 © 2006 Senn-Delaney Leadership Consulting Group, LLC.

Action Steps

When Senn-Delaney Leadership interviews clients to customize our culture-shaping seminars, people often tell us they are glad this is taking place because it is really needed to "fix" someone else on the team. In starting a session, we occasionally ask the question, "What will happen if we all are here in the hopes someone else will change?" The answer, of course, is nothing.

So, the best thing you can do in reading this book is to be willing to be a bit introspective and ask yourself, "How can I better live life at my best at work and at home?"

That is the greatest contribution you can make to a *winning team* and a *winning culture*.

3

SHADOW OF THE LEADER

"A leader doesn't just get the message, he is the message."

—*Warren Bennis*[19]

A few years ago, a CEO asked us if we could help shift one aspect of his company's culture. It was a strong culture in many ways. They had high performance expectations, committed hard-working employees, good basic values and fairly good performance. He felt they could go from good to great if they could collaborate better across the organization and get more synergies from the different business units. He and others on the senior team were aware that most organization-wide initiatives had fallen short of potential. Their shared services initiative didn't yield all it could have: A major IT installation took longer and cost more than expected and customers still couldn't get fully integrated solutions.

As we started the cultural diagnostics, it became clear that they did have some "we-they" and turf issues between corporate and business units and between different functions. While the CEO wanted us to help "fix" the organization, it didn't take long to see that the issues were largely a reflection of the senior team. They were not fully aligned or mutually supportive. They didn't speak with one voice to the organization. They were generally polite and non-confronting. They had a habit of appearing to agree on a decision in a meeting, but then not supporting the decision outside the meeting. As we dug deeper we found many of the same behaviors existed at the second level in the teams that reported to senior team members. We asked people at lower levels in the organization why they didn't collaborate better, and they said in various ways, "Why should we? Our bosses don't." To us the organization structure looked like the chart on the next page (Figure 3.1).

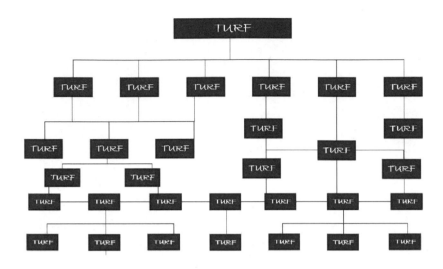

Figure 3.1 © 2006 Senn-Delaney Leadership Consulting Group, LLC.

Lack of collaboration is only one cultural trait impacted by the shadow of the leaders. You could substitute many things in the boxes above, including: *Blaming, Stress, Lack of Coaching, Resistance to Change, Hectic, Hierarchical, Risk-Averse, etc.*

The central finding of Larry Senn's doctoral dissertation on culture 35 years ago was that over time, organizations tend to take on the characteristics of their leaders. This was easy to see in the field studies that were conducted of smaller firms. The values, habits and biases of the founders and dominant leaders left an imprint on the organization. Today we can see this in the largest of corporations. It's clearly visible in companies like Wal-Mart, where Sam Walton had such a distinct impact on the culture. The impact Herb Kelleher had on Southwest Airlines is also apparent, as is the shadow that Jack Welch left at GE. The same is true in all organizations, at least from a historical perspective. There are often "ghosts" of past leaders evident. To better understand that, just ask about the values and preferences of dominant founders of a company, or early leaders who left their mark. Chances are you can still see at least remnants that have made an impact many years later. A good example is Walt Disney and Disney Theme Parks.

Because of the size and complexity of organizations today, the most important shadows come from teams at the top; specifically, the CEO's team and the teams of those that report to the CEO. Therefore, if you want to shape any element of your culture, your teams need to model the desired behavior.

THE SHADOW PHENOMENON

The phenomenon exists to greater or lesser degrees for anyone who is a leader of any group, including a parent in a family. That is because people tend to take on the characteristics of those that have some power or influence over them.

One of the most intimate and far-reaching examples of this shadow concept happens when parents, perhaps aware of their own imperfections, exhort their children to "Do as I say, not as I do." Unfortunately, children generally tune out that message and mimic the behaviors they see. The message of any parent, or business leader, will be drowned out if the actions conflict with the words.

> *"Children have never been very good at listening to their elders, but they have never failed to imitate them."*
>
> —*James Baldwin*
> *American author noted for his works on personal identity and civil rights*

Parenting is a huge responsibility, and too often we forget how our behaviors and attitudes affect our children. Henry Wheeler Shaw once said, "To bring up a child in the way he should go, travel that way yourself once in a while."

The role of the leader, at work and at home, requires modeling the desired behavior and letting others see the desired values in action. To become effective leaders, we must become aware of our shadows and then learn to have our actions match our message.

A former CEO of one Fortune 500 company felt so strongly about the importance of consistency between actions and words, he once said:

> *"I would submit to you that it is unnatural for you to come in late and for your people to come in early. I think it is unnatural for you to be dishonest and your people to be honest. I think it is unnatural for you to not handle your finances well and then to expect your people to handle theirs well. In all these simple things, I think you have to set the standard."*[20]

The head of an organization or a team casts a shadow that influences the employees in that group. The shadow may be weak or powerful, but it always exists. It is a reflection of everything the leader does and says. Marjorie M. Blanchard, co-founder of Blanchard Training and Development, Inc., describes it this way:

> *"People are smart. If you say one thing and do another, people see the discrepancies. Every decision I make as a leader in my company is being watched for the meaning and the values behind it. When you make a mistake, you create a negative story that can last a long time. So leaders have to lead by example, and be aware of the impact they create."[21]*

AN EXAMPLE OF THE "SHADOW IMPACT"

We learned a real-life lesson about the shadow of leaders early in the history of Senn-Delaney Leadership. J.L. Hudson, a division of one of the top U.S. department store companies, Dayton Hudson Corporation in Detroit (now Target Corporation), asked us to help them work on improving customer service in their stores, with the goal of becoming more like the high-end department store Nordstrom. We piloted the process in six stores working with the store managers, with mixed success. Some stores had measurable increases in service levels and increased market share, while others didn't. In fact, the results were almost directly proportional to our success in shifting the store manager's focus from operations to service, and his/her management style. It demonstrated how the leader's shadow of influence crossed the store. This is what we would later term "the shadow of the leader."

We concluded our mixed success was a result of starting at the wrong level in the organization; we discovered this in an interesting way. When we asked sales associates why they weren't more attentive or friendlier to customers, they would say (in different ways), "Who's friendly and attentive to me?" When we would ask their department managers the same question, we got the same answer. That continued on up through the assistant store manager, the store manager, the district manager, the vice president of stores, and on up to the executive committee. We concluded that fixing the stores was similar to family therapy; you have to include the parents.

Soon after, the CEO of The Broadway Department Stores in California, now a part of The Federated Department Stores company, asked if we would develop a customer service process for them, we politely said, "Only if we can begin with the executive committee." That led to several consecutive years of increased sales and market share for The Broadway.

All too often leaders in an organization approve of training programs dealing with issues such as leadership development or culture shaping, but don't attend them as participants or visibly work on the concepts themselves. More often than not, as a result, these programs are unsuccessful. That is why it is critical that any major change initiative, such as culture shaping, start at the top.

CULTURAL IMPLICATIONS OF THE SHADOW OF THE LEADER

One of the most common complaints throughout organizations is that the senior team is not "walking the talk." Whenever a company begins to make statements about desired behaviors, and people don't see those behaviors being modeled at the top, there is a lack of integrity. This can take various forms:

- The organization is asking people to be more open to change, yet the top leaders do not exhibit changed behaviors.

- Increased teamwork and cross-organizational collaboration is preached, yet the senior team does not collaborate across divisional lines.

- The organization is seen cutting back on expenses, yet the senior team doesn't change any of its special perks.

- People are asked to be accountable for results while the senior team members continue to subtly blame one another for lack of results.

We have found that the fastest way to create a positive self-fulfilling prophecy about cultural change is to have the top leaders individually and collectively shift their own behaviors. They don't have to be perfect, they just have to deal themselves into the same game they are asking others to play. When leadership, teambuilding and culture-shaping training are a part of the change process, the senior team should be the first team to take part. If 360° (multirater) feedback assessments (described in Chapter 15) or other instruments are used to measure behaviors, then the senior team should be the first to step up and be measured.

Anyone who has ever conducted training processes with middle management knows the limitations of starting at this level. When attendees are asked about the value of the session, the classic responses are, "My boss is the one who should be attending," or "It sounds great, but that's not the way it is around here; just look at my manager."

Because of the critical need for the senior team to role-model the new culture, they are the group that first needs to come together in a shared, offsite process to define the guiding behaviors for the rest of the organization. Whenever this is delegated to a committee under them, or to expert writers, the statements of values may read well, but are not owned by and don't reside in the hearts of the senior team. When the values don't live in the senior team, the probability that the organization will live the values is low.

As a firm that specializes in culture shaping, Senn-Delaney Leadership has an unwritten policy that we won't design or conduct a culture-shaping architecture for clients unless we can first work with the team that leads the organization, or a major semi-autonomous group, and its leader. It's not that we don't want the business; it's just that we know that without a positive leadership shadow, the process is unlikely to work.

In order to build a winning culture, the top teams must be seen by the organization as living the values and walking the talk. Based on the size of the organization, it is usually the top 100 to 500 people that really set the culture.

Action Steps

Some useful questions to ask yourself about the shadow concept are:

1. What shadow is the senior team(s) in your organization casting? What's the good news? And the bad news?

    very different from person to person

2. What behaviors would you like to see change in the group you lead or influence at work? Once identified, how do you have to show up differently to cast the needed shadow?

    more engaged different aspects of Cyber Core

3. If you have children or younger people you influence in your personal life, what are they learning and picking up on based upon your behaviors? What are your positive behaviors and what do you need to watch out for? What shadow do you want to cast?

4

WINNING TEAMS

The Eight Requirements of a Healthy, High-Performance Team

Since the *shadow of the leader* impact is so great, creating winning teams at the top is critical to creating a winning culture. When the top teams live the values and collaborate across the organization for the greater good, they provide a solid foundation for a healthy, high-performance culture.

The members of top teams in most organizations are usually talented and highly effective <u>individuals;</u> however, they often don't operate as an aligned, healthy, high-performance team. They may run their functions or specialties effectively, but they usually don't do as well in working together to guide the organization.

The Test

Maybe your team is an exception. One way to find out is to rank them objectively on how well they meet eight requirements of a healthy high-performance team. These guidelines are based on our work with hundreds of teams of Global 1000 companies over the past 25 years.

1. Do they make decisions unselfishly, for the greater good of the organization, or do they tend to make decisions in their own self-interest?

This "greater good" quality distinguishes the best leadership teams from collections of talented individuals. This is often most apparent at the top of the organization. For example, in a "holding company" business model, where business units operate for the most part as separate organizations, the game may be set up with a win-lose mindset—every group for themselves. If so, the same self-interest phenomenon is evident at all levels.

The focus may be on maximizing individual sub-unit performance, even if it results in unhealthy competition and reduces the company's overall economic value. In this environment, costs are generally higher because of duplicated services and a lack of economy of scale.

Most companies today realize the value in operating with a "shared services" business model. In doing so they hope to:

- Implement more cost-effective shared services.

- Gain more synergies between businesses.

- Present a more seamless face to the customer with bundled solutions.

- Use the senior team as a group of advisors in setting direction and helping one another.

This model can be very effective, if the leaders are truly committed to making decisions for the greater good.

2. Is your team seen by the organization as being aligned on goals and priorities?

Teams do best when everyone is pulling together in the same direction at the same time. People in organizations are very much attuned to the priorities of their leaders. When top leaders aren't aligned, it is obvious to everyone and chances are the organization below them will be unaligned as well.

Alignment does not mean that team members never voice dissent or disagree with a decision. In fact, in the best teams people do speak up when they have meaningful differences in point-of-view. Alignment means that when the team agrees on the importance of focusing the energy of the organization in one direction, its members are committed to behaving in a way that supports that focus, rather than distracts from it. Healthy teams work to gain and maintain alignment.

3. Do team members consistently "assume best intentions" in one another, or do they "assume motives" especially when they disagree?

Assuming motives in others takes people down the Mood Elevator; assuming best intentions helps keep people up the Mood Elevator. When teammates assume motives in one another, then discussions, communications, decisions and execution suffer. Very few people, if any, get up in the morning and say "I'm going to see how much damage I can do today." Most people are doing what makes sense to them. Most errors are unintentional. *even the dumb ones*

The problem is that when we assume ill intentions, we damage trust. Trust is the foundation of a healthy team. You build trust by being willing to assume that your teammates also want what they think is best for the organization. They may have vastly different opinions about exactly what that is, but with a foundation of trust, you can engage in open and respectful discussions of the issues. To the degree that a team can maintain this level of openness, they can learn from one another and find mutually beneficial solutions.

> 4. Do they openly discuss issues in meetings or do most "real" conversations take place in the hallways after the meetings?

Only the best teams have free, open, respectful yet challenging conversations in their meetings. In far too many companies, either the team leader is conflict-averse so no one wants to bring up the elephant they all know is in the room, or the unwritten rule is, "I won't comment on your sandbox if you don't comment on mine." These two factors create superficial, information-exchange-type meetings.

The connection to results was shown clearly in some data from the McKinsey & Co. study *The War for Talent*, which compared the top performing quintile of companies with the mid-quintile (not the lowest performing quintile). This study found that there was a dramatic difference in openness and candor in meetings between the two (Figure 4.1 next page).[22]

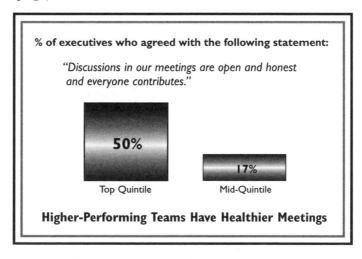

% of executives who agreed with the following statement:

"Discussions in our meetings are open and honest and everyone contributes."

50% — Top Quintile

17% — Mid-Quintile

Higher-Performing Teams Have Healthier Meetings

Figure 4.1 © 2006 Senn-Delaney Leadership Consulting Group, LLC. Extrapolated from "The War for Talent".

One of the companies surveyed by McKinsey & Co. was Home Depot. They have a great motto regarding meetings: "Say what you think in the room, not after the meeting."

5. When a decision is made in a senior team meeting, does everyone own the decision as theirs and fully support it outside the meeting room?

Yum! Brands' David Novak put together one of the better teams we've worked with. One of the team's mottos is, "Team Together, Team Apart." To them, that has a special meaning. Everyone openly dialogs and shares different points of view in meetings but once a decision is made, they speak with one voice to the organization in owning and implementing the decision.

"Team Together, Team Apart" at Yum! Brands also means that they support one another outside the meeting by helping each other be successful and never speaking negatively about one another. This mindset has kept Novak's company successful throughout many challenges over the years.

6. Do they all walk the talk by living the values (integrity)?

In all too many organizations, people look at the teams above them and see dysfunctions like lack of alignment on priorities, turf issues or little mutual support. In short, people don't see the team fully living the values and behaviors the company stands for. In most companies, ethics and integrity are solid, but there are other critical values that aren't modeled as well. For example, leaders may be seen as guarding turf rather than collaborating or not being open to changes that impact them. High-performance teams walk the talk by adhering to all the essential values—both when together and when apart. One measure of a great team is that the hallway talk is not about how people wish their senior team was. It is about how pleased they are with how the team shows up and the great shadow they cast. This is especially important for the next guideline:

7. Are they acutely aware of the impact their shadows cast?

Most leaders greatly underestimate the impact they have on the organization under them just by the way they show up. Everything from their words to their mood is noticed. Anyone who chooses to be a parent or a leader has a special obligation to understand that others who look up to them tend to emulate their behaviors. The top teams have the highest obligation because they have the most leverage and are most closely watched. If they are unaligned, the organization is probably unaligned as well. If they aren't seen as a team, there will probably be silos under them. If they don't coach, then coaching won't be a part of their organization's culture.

When business leaders understand the concept of shadow of the leader, the results can be powerful. Mary Foster, President of Sylvan Learning Centers, tells us, "One of the things that has been most empowering for people was for me to cast a shadow that coaching and learning begins with me—that I need it too. This was incredibly freeing for others, making it okay for everyone to acknowledge their own strengths and challenges and to focus on how to get better results. It's helping us improve our processes, our meeting effectiveness, our overall productivity and results. Even in our annual performance reviews, which could be rather uncomfortable for everyone, people now walk out inspired and happy to know what they are doing well and what they need to work on to be even more effective."

8. Do they fully participate in initiatives or do they just "bless" them?

Since leaders cast a long shadow, all really important organizational changes need to start with the top team. Whether the key initiative involves a new computer system or a new value system, a 360° (multi-rater) feedback assessment or leadership training, it needs to be <u>owned and used by the top team first.</u>

How does your team measure up to the previous eight questions? If your team normally displays these healthy behaviors, then keep up the good work! Your team and organization are sure to benefit. If not, perhaps your leadership team deserves some attention.

Even though the behaviors of the team at the top have a huge impact on a company, few teams spend the necessary quality time on their own development. It's like a sports team playing in a championship game without practice and without established plays. Fortunately, processes exist that can systematically and consistently improve the effectiveness of a senior team in these eight dimensions. Senior teams who do take time to work on becoming an even better team are able to tackle strategic issues with focus and alignment, and in so doing, achieve greater results for their organization while creating a stronger culture overall.

A Leverage Point for Winning Teams

Teams operate at different levels of the Mood Elevator (Figure 4.2), just as people do. If there is a leverage point for teams, it is managing their *collective* Mood Elevator.

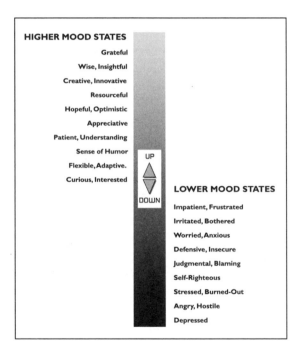

HIGHER MOOD STATES

Grateful

Wise, Insightful

Creative, Innovative

Resourceful

Hopeful, Optimistic

Appreciative

Patient, Understanding

Sense of Humor

Flexible, Adaptive.

Curious, Interested

UP

DOWN

LOWER MOOD STATES

Impatient, Frustrated

Irritated, Bothered

Worried, Anxious

Defensive, Insecure

Judgmental, Blaming

Self-Righteous

Stressed, Burned-Out

Angry, Hostile

Depressed

Figure 4.2 © 2006 Senn-Delaney Leadership Consulting Group, LLC.

It is difficult, if not impossible, for teammates to collaborate effectively when they are on the lower floors of the elevator, feeling self-righteous, judgmental, defensive or insecure. Conversely, it is easy to collaborate when feeling hopeful, optimistic, resourceful and flexible.

If you review the eight characteristics of a winning team, you will find that in each case the winning behaviors are natural and automatic when in a higher state of mind. In the higher states you:

- Are more selfless vs. selfish and more likely to make decisions for the greater good.

- Assume best intentions vs. motives in your teammates.

- Exhibit values like accountability, agility, integrity and teamwork.

- Listen better to other points of view and speak more directly to others.

- Are more supportive of others.

- Support team decisions more consistently.

If we understand the role of thought and moods and how they drive our behaviors, we can also avoid doing damage when we are in the lower states of mind. Our thinking is less reliable in the lower mood states so anger is not the best place to come from when delivering a message. It produces the kind of comments you later wish you hadn't said.

If all your teammates have some understanding of these principles, you can become more aligned, have more productive meetings and cast the kind of shadow you want on the organization, because you will be a winning team. And, you will have a solid foundation for a winning culture, since a winning culture is a collection of winning teams collaborating for the greater good.

Action Steps

1. Consider the teams you belong to: both the team you lead and any team of which you are a member. On which of the eight items in the "test" do your teams perform well?

   college does not do any of them very well.
   There's an effort to make decisions for
   the overall good however at the
   Deans/chairs level.

2. Which of the eight items need most improvement?

   Assuming best intentions
   support decisions outside the meeting

3. Ask your teammates to do the same thing, and compare and discuss your views.

5

A PROVEN CULTURE-SHAPING MODEL

ALL ORGANIZATIONS HAVE CULTURES. THE ONLY QUESTION IS, DO YOU SHAPE IT OR DOES IT SHAPE YOU?

Can leaders actually reshape the culture of an organization?

That was the question we faced when we started this journey over 25 years ago. We knew it was possible in smaller companies, with strong enough leaders at the top casting clear and positive shadows. It had also been done in larger companies with powerful enough "burning platforms." However, the successes were rare, since more companies had failed than succeeded. Many have created programs that have faded too soon. Others have launched culture shaping initiatives that became "the flavor of the month (or year)" but didn't stick.

This has been true of:

- Culture-shaping initiatives to support business transformation.

- Broad-based leadership development programs.

Many of the ideas in this book were discovered while gaining an understanding of why those initiatives failed and, conversely, what it took to measurably shift a culture. Some of the most common reasons initiatives failed include:

- The change initiative may have been endorsed by the leader or senior team but was not led or modeled by them (the shadow of the leader).

- Values and behaviors were created, but were not comprehensive enough to truly define the desired culture.

- Values were created and hung on the walls, but no process was used to help people truly internalize the behaviors and make a deep personal commitment to change. The desired behaviors were deployed as a communications process or in meetings where they were discussed but not internalized. They were not "lived" by people in the organization.

- The leadership development or culture shaping process became one of many "disconnected initiatives." Not all HR systems were aligned to the new values. People may have been hired to one criterion, rewarded on another and measured by 360° multirater surveys on another—but none were fully aligned with each other or the specific desired cultural behaviors.

- The process did not reach a critical mass of people or move fast enough to overcome the inertia of the existing culture.

- Leadership and team-effectiveness training were not conducted in natural work groups with a leader. Instead, people went to classes in mixed groups or high-potential executives were sent off to institutions of higher education. When those people went back to their natural work group, the habits and norms of the culture overcame much of what had been taught in the sessions.

- Leadership development was seen as a "nice to do" not a "have to do," because it was not connected to real business issues.

- No process was set up to measure improvements in behaviors or results. Without proof of gains the process died an early death.

Senn-Delaney Leadership made some of the same mistakes in the early years. The example we cited in Chapter 3 of our work at J.L. Hudson department store is a case in point. We tried to create a service culture by engaging the store organization but not the CEO and senior team. Without having the merchants, IT, supply chain and others on board the results were mixed.

Some of our greatest lessons have come in our work to transform the culture of a regional phone company—Bell Atlantic (who later merged with NYNEX and GTE to become Verizon). We were fortunate to start with strong active leadership by the CEO, Ray Smith. He helped us understand the impact of a leader who had an unwavering commitment to the change process. He and his entire office group devoted days of time offsite to define and internalize the new Bell

Atlantic Way values and to understand the shadow they cast. Smith's story and the Bell Atlantic Way are detailed in Chapter 7.

The major mistake we made was in the initial architecture for deployment of the values. Because the old phone companies were very hierarchical and level-conscious, and they had a strong desire to break down silos, we agreed with their request to do mixed groups from across the organization at each level after the senior team. It soon became apparent that by not working with a leader and his or her team, we could not get the day-to-day, person-to-person reinforcement, and the groups could not apply their learnings to the specific business issues of their group. When we backtracked and shifted to a team-learning model with intact teams and natural work groups, momentum grew and the shift began to take place. Ultimately major shifts were made in the three characteristics the CEO knew were needed to lead the industry: collaboration vs. turf, accountability vs. entitlement and agility vs. bureaucracy.

THE CHANGE MODEL

Our experiences over the years have led to the creation of a five-step model for systematically shaping behaviors of leaders, teams and overall cultures. When that model is applied in the right sequence to the right groups, measurable changes in behaviors occur. We call this model DURAM™, based on the initials of the 5 steps (Figure 5.1).

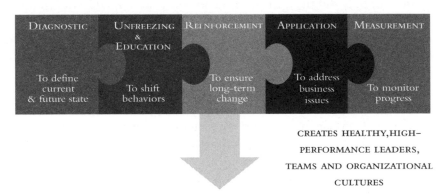

DIAGNOSTIC	UNFREEZING & EDUCATION	REINFORCEMENT	APPLICATION	MEASUREMENT
To define current & future state	To shift behaviors	To ensure long-term change	To address business issues	To monitor progress

CREATES HEALTHY, HIGH-PERFORMANCE LEADERS, TEAMS AND ORGANIZATIONAL CULTURES

SUSTAINABLE RESULTS

Figure 5.1 © 2006 Senn-Delaney Leadership Consulting Group, LLC.

While each element is not totally self-contained, there is a general sequence:

1. **D**iagnose the existing culture and business needs and **Define** the desired culture.

2. **U**nfreeze the old dysfunctional behaviors and connect people to the new desired behaviors through insight-based training.

3. **R**einforce the new behaviors by aligning all HR systems and providing ongoing reinforcement for all individuals.

4. **A**pply the new behaviors to improving business results.

5. **M**easure progress for individuals, teams and the organization.

THE CULTURAL TRANSFORMATION OF TENNESSEE VALLEY AUTHORITY

The Tennessee Valley Authority (TVA) story is a great example of an organization that applied the DURAM™ model correctly and successfully. It has done so in a way that created one of the most cost-effective and reliable energy systems in the world.

Some years ago their chairman, presidential appointee Craven Crowell, and his team concluded that in order to better fulfill the vision of TVA, they needed to transform the culture. TVA has played an important historic role in the economic development of its seven-state region. Not only did they produce the power that helped to develop that region, but also maintained its waterways.

With approaching deregulation and a desire to be even more self-sufficient, there was a need to produce lower-cost power with high reliability and safety. This was a challenge because the organization is a pseudo-governmental one in that the chairman and full-time operating board who manage TVA are political appointees, the employees operate under a civil service system and the organization is largely unionized. While TVA has a dedicated and committed workforce, internal surveys indicated that its culture was not ideal. As in many organizations, especially those with long histories and a protected market, there were turf issues and silos, somewhat of an entitlement mindset and a fair degree of resistance to change.

Today, all measurable indicators of cultural behaviors and organizational performance have improved. Currently, TVA's nuclear plants are among the world's top performers in terms of cost, liability and safety. TVA's nuclear plants are some of the few that have received the highest rating possible from the Institute of Nuclear Power Operations, INPO 1. Their fossil and hydro plants have also set records for productivity.

TVA's culture-shaping process followed the five steps in the DURAM™ model. They began with diagnostics to better understand the existing culture and define the desired culture. With these goals in mind, they named the process STAR 7, derived from the fact that they served seven states and developed seven values to define their new culture (Figure 5.2)[23].

TVA's Values

VALUES TVA

To achieve a position of leadership, TVA relies on leaders at all levels who continuously strive to exceed the Goals, energetically communicate the Vision, and live (or model) the following Seven Values aimed at Strategic Teamwork for Action and Results:

Integrity
Value actions that are fair, responsible, and proper above all else. Conduct all activities according to the highest ethical standards and measures of social responsibility.

Respect for the Individual
Recognize that everyone — and everyone's work — is important and that managing and utilizing diversity are keys to business success. Give the responsibility, authority, training, and tools necessary to make decisions to the person closest to the internal or external customer.

Accountability
Take responsibility for our own assigned tasks and the performance of our workgroup, plant, and TVA. Focus on ownership versus blaming when encountering setbacks. Demonstrate a can-do attitude by taking initiative.

Teamwork
Value working cooperatively with others towards what is needed to get "the job done for TVA" —not on "what is my job."

Innovation and Continuous Improvement
Foster an atmosphere that values quality, constant improvement, and creativity; encourages prudent risktaking; and uses mistakes as an opportunity for learning.

Honest Communication
Establish effective, honest, and open communication among all employees, business units, and customers to improve TVA's effectiveness.

Flexibility
Be quick and flexible in responding to new opportunities and meeting customers' needs. Embrace necessary change.

STAR
★★★★★★★
SEVEN

Figure 5.2 TVA Star 7 Values.

These values were one result of the initial three-day unfreezing seminar with the chairman and senior team. Similar Star 7 seminars were carried throughout the organization in intact teams, to unfreeze old behaviors and connect people to the Star 7 guiding behaviors.

All of TVA's reinforcement systems, performance management systems and compensation systems were revised to be consistent with the Star 7 values. A robust internal communications program, including a Star 7 newsletter, was created to provide additional reinforcement.

The values were connected to business results through a process TVA called *Translating Values to Action* (also aptly called TVA). Each work group or team did pre-work to connect their goals to the overall corporate goals in a process they called "line of sight." Next, their Star 7 facilitators assist senior line managers in conducting a second round of "unfreezing" workshops designed to both reinforce Star 7 behaviors and gain commitment to performance improvement in each of the areas that had "line of sight."

Being a regulated utility, TVA excels at measurement. They've set up one of the most comprehensive cultural audit programs we've ever seen, which provides information on how each function, plant and work group is performing relative to the guiding behaviors that define the Star 7 values. In addition, they measure progress at an individual level through a 360° (multirater) feedback assessment, called the Guiding Behaviors Inventory process.

One of the organization's desires as they began the process was to create something powerful enough that it would endure, and not change with each political administration. When Bush succeeded Clinton, Glenn McCullough was appointed Chairman of TVA to succeed Craven Crowell. He and the other new board members reviewed the process and not only approved it, but re-engaged the organization at an even deeper level with the Star 7 Values.

Principles of Culture Shaping

Embedded in Senn-Delaney Leadership's DURAM™ model are some principles of shaping a culture, including:

1. Start at the top since organizations become shadows of their leaders. This is important because unless people see the senior team leading and modeling the change, the process is unlikely to be fully successful.

2. Understand and face up to the current dysfunctions in the culture, and define the desired end state via values and behaviors.

3. Use insight-based seminars to connect people emotionally, not just intellectually, to the desired values and behaviors.

4. Have groups come together for training as intact teams or natural work groups, not unrelated managers.

5. Support the new learning with ongoing, comprehensive and integrated reinforcement.

6. Have the intact team apply what they learn to real business issues.

7. Measure behavior changes for people, teams and the organization.

There is one other often overlooked secret of shaping a culture:

Overwhelm the Old Culture by Moving Quickly and Achieving Critical Mass.

Cultures have a great deal of inertia and are very resilient. Slow moving and half-hearted efforts to change them, such as communication programs, are unlikely to succeed on their own, because they don't provide people with a gut-level connection to the need for change. Therefore, once the senior team has defined the new behaviors and begun to work on them themselves, levels under them need to go through their own insight-based unfreezing, reinforcement and applications efforts as quickly as possible. An extreme example of this is the rebirth of KFC.

When Yum! Brands Chairman, CEO and President David Novak took over the KFC organization, one of his first goals was rapid improvement in sales within the restaurants and a new relationship with the franchise organization. Both had been damaged over the years under former leaders and owners. Novak started at the top by having the senior team take quality time to define the elements of their "How We Work Together" Principles. Next, key corporate functions in the support center were brought on board to begin to demonstrate that corporate was really there to help. Then, an unusual "mega-session" strategy was selected for the restaurant organization. More than 3,000 restaurant general managers came to Louisville for a week to take part in an insight-based unfreezing workshop modeled after the one in which the senior team and support center had participated. They learned about values and behaviors and were also introduced to some key improvement processes for the restaurants, called the Baker's Dozen.

The organization created significant same-store sales gains in the following months and got back on a winning track. Novak used creative forms of reinforcement to create a winning culture based largely on employee and customer recognition. While the large group intervention approach was unusual, it illustrates the importance of moving quickly to gain critical mass in changing behaviors. The process, which Senn-Delaney Leadership facilitated for KFC, is described in the book *Customer Mania* by Ken Blanchard, Jim Ballard, and Fred Finch.[24]

What may not be apparent is the fact that utilizing an integrated and comprehensive process of change, like the DURAM™ model described here, is one of the secrets to success in and of itself. That's because all too often the shortfall is due to slow-moving, disconnected initiatives.

Action Steps

Each of the elements in the DURAM™ model is described in more detail in the following chapters. The next two chapters cover ways to diagnose your culture and your team. As you read through each chapter, we urge you to ask yourself how you can take advantage of the principles that are described.

DIAGNOSING YOUR OWN CULTURE

Figure 6.1 © 2006 Senn-Delaney Leadership Consulting Group, LLC.

Understanding Your Culture: the Fitness Model vs. the Medical Model

While a few of our clients come to us because they have extremely dysfunctional cultures, the vast majority don't. Most have sound cultures and core values. They are looking to shift their cultures, not because they are broken, but because they want to be the best they can be: to move from good to great.

In all those cases, we liken our work to a *fitness model* vs. a *medical model*. It's like a person who decides they want to get in better shape and improve some aspect of their fitness *before* they have their coronary problems, not after.

Prior to a fitness improvement program, it is important to run diagnostics to determine what you want or need to improve. As individuals, especially after a certain age, we are encouraged to get a complete physical periodically. Tools and specialists are available to help with this.

> *LARRY*: I travel to Cooper Clinic in Dallas every few years to get a comprehensive executive physical. Ken Cooper, who founded

the clinic, is a specialist in diagnostics. He is internationally renowned as "the father of aerobics" and has done extensive work to demonstrate the connection between cardiovascular fitness and exercise.

The Cooper diagnostics include a wide range of tests, including blood chemistry—cholesterol and all its components, PSA for prostate health, stress tests on treadmills, underwater weighing for body fat content, strength and flexibility testing, and lung capacity. The comprehensive report provides specific advice on areas to work on to increase my level of fitness.

In a like manner, the first step in any culture shaping is to begin by understanding the strengths as well as the challenges in your team or your culture.

What are the values that have contributed to your success that you want to strengthen or retain? What are the organizational habits you need to change in order to move to a higher level of performance?

When we meet leaders, many are already fairly clear about what they like in the culture of their organization, and what they want to see changed. For instance, Ray Smith clearly understood that the monopolistic history of phone companies had created a very procedurally driven, rule-oriented culture at Bell Atlantic (before it merged with GTE to become Verizon). The historic vision of dependable, universal service and cost-plus pricing had created an engineering-dominated, perfectionist culture. In this culture, systems were, as Smith said, "gold-plated" to last for decades, but not necessarily innovative from a customer standpoint. Because of the stability that industry had enjoyed for many years, employees felt very safe and had more of a sense of entitlement than a feeling of accountability or bias for action. Because they were organized by each state with no outside competition, they were internally competitive. The result was a siloed, turf-based culture.

In most organizations, it is useful to gather the data to confirm anecdotal evidence and help build a case for change. In Bell Atlantic/Verizon's case, the needs of the organization were clear: more accountability, teamwork and more agility. Because of this, Smith didn't need a lot of data to build a case for change. However, the data we did gather served to confirm what he already knew and helped him solidify his direction. There is more on Smith's story in Chapter 7.

In most cases cultural diagnostics are essential because companies suffer from some degree of familiarity blindness. The executives are so used to the long-standing habits that they don't notice them anymore, like the concept of unhealthy normal we discussed in Chapter 2 on personal transformation.

There are a number of formal and informal ways to gain a better understanding of the strengths and challenges of your culture for both such purposes. It is important to be aware that traditional survey data has limitations.

Why Most Employee Surveys Don't Tell the Real Story

In many companies, employee surveys exist, and it would seem that enough data describing the culture is already available. However, **there is often a problem with existing data**.

Most employee surveys focus on how people "feel" or how they are treated, but not on *how people behave* in the culture. For the purposes of culture shaping, it is less important to know if people like the compensation system and benefits than if they have a "can-do" attitude and high level of accountability. For that reason, while useful for other purposes, these surveys don't tell the real story behind the organization's culture.

The kinds of questions the surveys *should* be asking include:

- Do different functions and business units tend to cooperate or compete? What "we-they" relationships exist?

- Is more effort spent on internal competition or external?

- Is there passive acceptance of ideas in meetings and aggressive resistance by management after meetings?

- Are managers able to successfully deal with conflict?

- When a goal or deadline is missed, or a result not accomplished, do people tend to make excuses and blame others, or are they highly accountable?

- Is it OK to make a mistake around here, or do you need to avoid all risk or cover it up?

- Does the organization tend to be hierarchical and level conscious? Can you bypass a boss to talk to someone higher up without committing a cultural "crime"?

- Do people tend to have a strong work ethic?

- Are there high levels of stress and burnout? Or do we have a healthy, fast pace?

- Are we customer-focused or operations-focused? What is our customer service experience really like?

- Does the culture tend to encourage new ideas or shoot them down?

- Are issues openly discussed in meetings, or afterwards in the hall?

- What are the current levels of trust and openness in the organization?

- Are people willing to constructively confront or are they passive/aggressive?

When a senior team of a company or unit does this kind of informal assessment of the culture, it can lead to healthy dialog about the strengths and challenges in the culture and the impact on strategies and initiatives. One format is to take a critical strategic initiative and honestly ask the question, "What qualities in our culture support success of that initiative *and* what habits or traits in our culture may defeat it or slow it down?

Here are some other tips for performing an informal assessment on your organization's culture:

- If you have a stated set of values, which ones are lived and which are not?

- Step back from your own view of the business; try to be objective.

- Since newer employees have a fresher viewpoint, ask them what they notice.

- Talk to employees with whom you don't normally interact.

- Make a list of company jokes and often-told stories; there is usually more truth than humor in them.

- Sit back and observe the human dynamics in a meeting, without focusing on the content. How do people behave?

- Observe the behavior of the senior team; their shadow *will* influence the culture.

A Proven Tool to Assess a Culture—The Corporate Culture Profile™

To fully understand your current culture, it is helpful to do an independent cultural audit. This differs from an employee attitude or satisfaction survey. A cultural audit will provide an outside impartial view of your culture to illustrate your company's healthy and unhealthy cultural behaviors and the motivational factors behind them. It will also establish what impact leadership has on the culture and whether the culture will support or hinder your strategic initiatives. By performing the diagnostic analysis, you can clearly define the path forward and establish a baseline measurement to evaluate progress.

We have found great value in using a specialized web-based survey that we developed to help clients get a clear and useful handle on their culture, called the Corporate Culture Profile™ (CCP). The CCP uses a seven-point scale to measure seven key characteristics within the culture. The first two questions measure alignment. How clear are people on the mission, strategy and key goals of the organization and how well is the senior team aligned?

+ Alignment

The other six categories are:

- Performance orientation

- Teamwork and collaboration

- Openness to change

- Ethics and integrity

- Organizational health, as measured by things like openness, trust and positive energy

- Service or commitment to customers

A work group or team, usually beginning with the entire senior team, is asked to complete the profile. They mark their perceptions of the strength of a trait on a scale like the one shown on page 21. The sample can be as small as the senior team or as large as the entire company. After over 25 years of normative data, we are comfortable with the profile's accuracy in identifying cultural traits, even with a small sample. It can, of course, be used with large populations; within one multi-national organization, a CCP was administered to 18,000 employees from various levels in a dozen different countries.

An Example

The client profile we will examine here (Figures 6.2 – 6.4) is an older, moderately successful, large insurance/financial services firm. A new CEO was appointed and committed to moving the company's performance from "good to great." Our cultural diagnosis almost always shows a story when looking at the high-scoring characteristics vs. the low-scoring ones (Figure 6.3). The story for this organization, as with all groups, was that they did have some historic strengths to build on. As a stable older traditional organization with a great work ethic and high integrity, their scores were highest in the categories of performance expectations, core values and ethics, customer service consciousness and integrity.

The challenges the new CEO faced were also clear in the data. The lowest scores (ones we call "in the red") included lack of teamwork, turf issues, low trust, hierarchical management, resistance to change and bureaucracy. The scores also showed that people were not clear enough on the organization's strategy and goals, and the senior team was not well aligned.

The forced-choice rankings (Figure 6.4) which asks survey participants to choose the top three strengths and three areas "most needed to improve," confirmed the story contained in the low and high scores but added one: lack of alignment at the top as a "most need to improve."

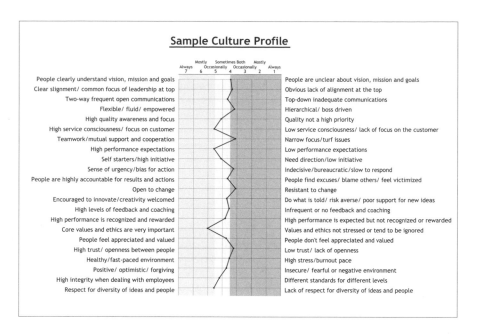

Figure 6.2 © 2006 Senn-Delaney Leadership Consulting Group, LLC.

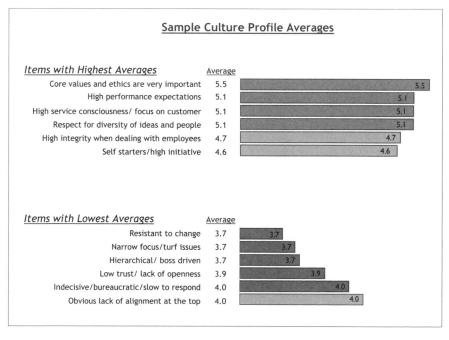

Figure 6.3 © 2006 Senn-Delaney Leadership Consulting Group, LLC.

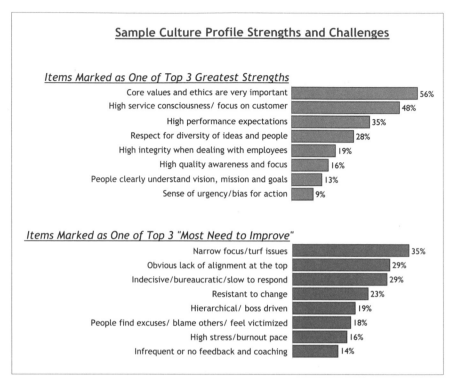

Figure 6.4 © 2006 Senn-Delaney Leadership Consulting Group, LLC.

Qualitative Analysis

The data clearly showed that this client needed improvement in the areas of change, alignment at the top and teamwork. One-on-one structured interviews, focus groups, and an understanding of both the industry and the company history brought added life to the data. In the company described here, the organization had a long history and tenured management team with a solid work ethic, which helped explain the high scores on high-performance expectations and ethical core values.

It also explained the hierarchical nature of the firm. They enjoyed a special market niche in one major business unit, which helped explain the reluctance to change and their slowness to respond. They were very polite and a bit passive-aggressive, so people tended to make excuses for shortfalls, rather than holding one another accountable or coaching each other.

The company had three major business units and had been operated largely in a holding company model, which explained the turf issues. Because their products historically had longer life cycles (compared to technology, for example) they were not as used to change and tended to resist it. Since they had at one time been a lifetime employment firm, people played it safe and avoided conflict to stay in favor and move up the ladder. The result was a risk-averse, hierarchical, boss-led culture.

DIAGNOSING THE CULTURE RELATIVE TO BUSINESS ISSUES

The purpose of a healthy high-performance culture is to support the long-term success of the business. It needs to drive business results and create a fulfilling place to work. In shaping a culture, it is important to know what strategies, business goals and initiatives the organization's behaviors need to support.

In the case of the insurance/financial services profile shown here, the CEO had a vision. He wanted a shared business model, not a holding company. He wanted more product innovation and greater speed to market. He believed that business growth and cost efficiencies could result from finding the synergies between the business units, and by using shared services vs. duplicated functions.

The CCP data was presented to the CEO and senior team in the form shown here, with a customized "jaws of culture" diagram (Figure 6.6, below) showing their initiatives. The changes in culture were apparent. The CEO had to align the team at the top around a clear shared vision of the direction and priorities of the business. To execute his strategy, he needed more cross-organizational collaboration, a greater bias for action and other key cultural drivers. The data from the culture assessment interviews and the CCP was convincing enough evidence for management to move more aggressively on reshaping the culture to support their business-change initiatives.

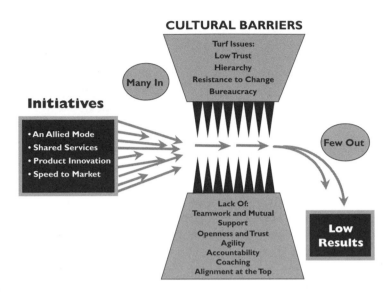

Figure 6.6 © 2006 Senn-Delaney Leadership Consulting Group, LLC.

The Nature of the Situation Dictates the Cultural Qualities Needed

The nature of the strategy or change initiatives underway is what dictates the qualities crucial to the culture. For example:

- If a business is moving toward use of shared services and common IT systems, then openness to change, teamwork and decisions for the greater good become critical.

- If the business is struggling to make its numbers, personal accountability for results and a "can-do" attitude are crucial to success.

- If top-line growth by adding market share from satisfied customers is needed, then a stronger external customer focus with added trust and improved quality and service awareness is essential.

Common Findings

We have completed and analyzed hundreds of CCPs for organizations. Highlights of the more generic and interesting generalizations include:

- Scores in the category of <u>stress levels and burnout</u> have been rising over the past five years. More people are feeling overwhelmed and dealing with balance-in-life issues. ↑

- High stress levels are almost always accompanied by low scores in <u>appreciation</u> and "high performance expected but not recognized." Conversely, stress levels are usually lower when employees feel appreciated, valued and recognized, irrespective of the workload. ↕

- Classic older institutions, as might be expected, often have less sense of urgency, more turf, more bureaucratic tendencies, and more blaming and excuses vs. accountability. The CCP helps them measure progress as they shift these tendencies over time.

- Younger growing organizations tend to have a greater sense of urgency and innovation, but often have burnout and lack of feedback and appreciation.

- People's intentions and work ethic usually score fairly high. The score that is <u>consistently the highest</u> is "high performance expectations"; i.e., most people want to perform well, and are expected to perform well to win.

- <u>Coaching and feedback</u> is consistently one of <u>the lower scores</u>. Most organizations do not have feedback-rich coaching cultures, so their ability to quickly adapt to changes suffers.

- Far too many large organizations are <u>not aligned as a team</u> at the top or around their strategies. This leads to wasted energy and resources as the leadership pursues multiple strategies at all levels that are not clear or aligned.

The Role of the Senior Leadership Team

More often than not the profile of the senior team and the organization have the same highs and lows. This validates the shadow of the leader principle.

Usually senior leaders look at the results of a companywide CCP and want to change specific cultural trait in the organization. The starting point is for the senior team to begin with their own individual and collective behaviors. Until they recognize *they* must be the first to change, there will be little, if any, success in shaping the overall company culture.

So, if you want to change your culture, measure your senior team first and begin the change process there.

Questions to Consider

1. What's the story in your culture? What are the cultural strengths you have to build on? What behaviors need to change most to ensure success for your company?

    strengths - v. high work ethic, expertise
    Δ - working together as a team

2. How about your own team? What habits or behaviors are getting in the way?

    not working together as a team.

7

ALIGNING STRATEGY, STRUCTURE AND CULTURE

"First we shape our institutions, and afterwards they shape us."

—*Winston Churchill*

Most leaders want to reshape aspects of their cultures to better drive business results. To do this, you need to diagnose your culture with your strategy as well as your organizational structure and processes in mind. Before you can create a culture that supports your change efforts, it's important to understand that a culture that works well under one set of business conditions can lead to failure when times and circumstances change. Therefore, you must first look at the relationship between strategy, organizational structure and culture.

- **Strategy** as used here can represent a business' core strategy such as the low cost, no-frills, comfortable-travel strategy found at Jet Blue; or strategic initiatives like growth through acquisitions, new product innovation or global expansion.

- **Structure** represents the organizational structure and model such as a holding company, allied business model or integrated business. It also represents the systems and processes in a firm.

- **Culture** is the collective habits and behaviors of all the teams and individuals that make up the organization.

Another way to view the elements is as: 1) goals and direction, 2) processes and 3) people. If you want the highest performance, then you must align all of them.

Senn-Delaney Leadership has used this Strategy, Structure, Culture Model extensively with clients to help them understand how change and culture interact, and how corporate culture often acts as a barrier to strategic change.

Aligning Strategy, Structure and Culture

Unless your culture supports your strategies, you will find it difficult to implement what is needed to meet increased competition or changes in the marketplace. In fact, if new strategies are dramatically different from the old, the culture is likely to conflict with the new direction. The new strategies will be ignored or sabotaged and will generally fail. If your culture is firmly embedded, you will find change difficult as the culture reinforces and perpetuates the status quo. Thus, the challenge of change is to shift the culture into alignment with the new strategy.

In the early stages of an organization, a culture that is supportive of the organization's strategy and structure often emerges (Figure 7.1). One author insightfully describes culture as "a group's shared learning as it struggles to survive in its environment; it is the solution to external and internal problems that has worked consistently for a group..."[25] Thus, culture develops over time, evolving in response to the demands of the internal and external environment and the behaviors of an organization's leadership. While early cultures are relatively flexible and formative, they harden and take on entrenched behaviors as leadership patterns become routine, structure builds up and processes form around it.

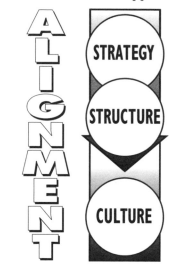

Figure 7.1 © 2006 Senn-Delaney Leadership Consulting Group, LLC.

In the retail industry, for example, it is easy to see this model in action. Wal-Mart pursues a mass-merchandising discount strategy, while Nordstrom depends on a strategy of providing a full line of soft goods with a significant focus on extraordinary customer service. Both Wal-Mart and Nordstrom are large, nationwide organizations that have been able to evolve strong cultures that are in alignment with their respective strategies, structures and systems. Their founding leaders also pursued behaviors that helped shape these cultures. Wal-Mart's Sam Walton focused on low cost of operations, an efficient supply chain and distribution system and positive energy in the stores.

In contrast, the Nordstrom family leaders came from a retail shoe sales culture where personal attention was required in fitting someone's shoes. As they became an apparel retail store, that same personal attention carried over. The culture became that of sales associates doing legendary things to satisfy a customer's needs.

Many industry observers agree that it is the strength of the Wal-Mart and Nordstrom cultures, which are very different yet equally strong, that make both organizations able to implement plans better than their competitors. While the competition may pursue similar strategies, they do so with less aligned or cohesive corporate cultures and achieve less impressive results. Wal-Mart and Nordstrom developed completely different strategies, structures and cultures, yet each organization is a highly aligned and productive organization with a vital competitive advantage.

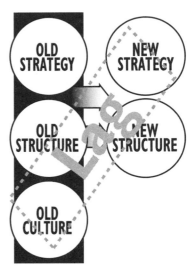

Figure 7.2 © 2006 Senn-Delaney Leadership Consulting Group, LLC.

Whenever an organization faces changes in its business environment, survival and prosperity depend on its ability to quickly change directions. Generally this involves a shift in strategy followed by changes in organizational structure (Figure 7.2).

As new strategies are developed and new structures put into place, many employees continue to think and perform in ways that were developed within the old culture. These cultural habits and methods of working and managing are often at odds with the new strategy and organizational structure. While the goals have shifted, the old ways of doing business are still in place and may now be in conflict with the company's new directives.

Here are some of the signs to look for that indicate a corporate culture has gotten out of alignment with the organization's strategy and structure:

- Frequent reorganizations to get people to work together more productively, but the turf issues still persist. ("It's in the DNA.")

- A need for innovation is clear, but the culture is risk-averse and employees don't feel empowered.

- Change in response to competition is imperative, but the culture is resistant to new ways of doing things.

✳ - New programs are discounted because of prior failed initiatives. ("We tried something like that before.")

- A strategy is developed to provide integrated solutions to customers, but the culture is based on protecting turf.

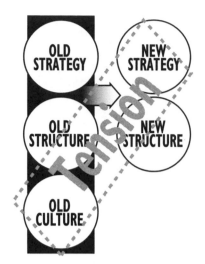

Figure 7.3 © 2006 Senn-Delaney Leadership Consulting Group, LLC.

- Numbers are missed while people spend time blaming or proving it's not their fault.

✳ - We agree to move forward in meetings, but then the participants go off and "do their own thing," i.e., passive/aggressive behavior.

In an organization that is out of alignment, more and more effort is required to make things work as the organization struggles to meet the challenges of today with the attitudes of yesterday. The result is often tension, resistance, passive/aggressive behavior and lowered morale instead of an effective, dynamic organization moving toward its goals. (Figure 7.3).

The old culture anchors the organization in the past, preventing it from moving forward. This creates an increasing level of frustration that peaks when some employees buy into the new way, while others remain mired in the old. It's like trying to sail a boat while dragging the anchor.

The challenge of leadership is to shape the culture so it is aligned with the

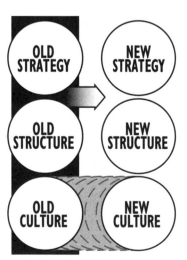

Figure 7.4 © 2006 Senn-Delaney Leadership Consulting Group, LLC.

new strategy and structure. We like to think in terms of *shaping* a culture as opposed to changing it, since cultural characteristics exist that should be retained and nurtured, while new characteristics will need to be added to make the culture more compatible with the new strategic thrust (Figure 7.4).

A "Universal" Example — The Creation of Verizon

Verizon was named the telecommunications industry's "Most Admired Company" by *Fortune* magazine in 2005[26]. It is one of the phone industry's survivors of divestiture, during which most regional "Bells," or local phone companies, and even AT&T itself, were acquired. Verizon's past two CEO's would attribute a portion of their success to the work they did to shape a winning culture. Its story is an interesting example of the power of culture and the importance of systematically shaping it.

In the telecommunications industry, AT&T was "Ma Bell" up until its 1984 breakup, which heralded the end of an era. The breakup created many regional Bells, while AT&T kept the long-distance business, plus the Bell Labs research arm. Today, the old AT&T exists in name only as part of SBC for global branding reasons.

Verizon has thrived in part because based upon our first-hand experience, it was the first phone company to recognize the need for cultural change, and act on it. Ray Smith had been part of the Bell system as Bell of Pennsylvania's CEO before moving up to the newly formed parent company, Bell Atlantic. Although he had grown up in the system, he was a visionary and an unconventional maverick in many ways. When he became Bell Atlantic's chairman and CEO, he recognized the need to drastically change the culture and implement new competitive strategies. Not long after meeting him, he described the situation to us in a very graphic metaphor: *"If I put my ear on the railroad track, I can hear a train coming our way and we are not prepared for what it is bringing."*[27]

What the train was bringing was competition to a monopolistic culture. The Bell Telephone System is a classic example of the effect of a changing industry on the alignment of strategy, structure and culture. For more than half a century, providing "universal service, end-to-end," with a reliability rate of 99.999%, was the Bell corporate vision, and they were very good at it. Every component in the organization—financial policies, technology, pricing philosophy, product and market strategies and organizational design—evolved to support that vision.

The Bell System's strategies were driven by regulatory and technological considerations. Financial policies were geared toward dividends, with a heavy debt structure and extensive external financing. Bell Laboratories, insulated in the regulated environment, was able to focus on basic research and technological opportunity without worrying about consumer preferences. Customer pricing, which was subsidized by the rate base, was based on the premise that everyone should be able to afford phone service. Marketing and product strategies focused on mass markets and standardized products. The corporate structure was large, centralized, bureaucratic and organized by function and geography.

The Bell culture included a regulatory mindset that favored adherence to policies and procedures, rigorous analysis of new projects and changes, and an elaborate approval process. The reward system fostered lifetime careers with a slow, steady progression and a strong focus on hierarchy. The culture—dedication to customer service, standardized procedures, loyalty and formal communication—was ideally aligned with the organization's structure and strategy of universal service.

W. Brooke Tunstall, an AT&T vice president who was closely involved in the divestiture planning leading up to the breakup of AT&T, provides an inside view of the cultural dynamics at AT&T in his book *Disconnecting Parties*:

> *"All these (cultural) attributes evolved to directly support one super-ordinate goal, universal service. In fact, everything related to the culture was affected by this goal; the kind of people we hired, their shared value systems, the infrastructure of processes to run the business. All were committed to the unchanging objective of providing high-quality service at affordable prices to everyone in the United States. Rarely, in fact, had corporate mission and corporate culture been so ideally matched."[28]*

That was not a culture prepared for a more competitive and innovative world. Smith saw three primary cultural habits that needed improvement:

- **Individual Accountability**—Employees felt victimized by divestiture, and spent too much time finger-pointing and blaming. They were good at *responding* to crises, such as service outages due to storms, but poor at *initiating* improvements. There were too many excuses and little proactive work on improving processes and performance. It was a classic entitlement mindset that would fail in the new game.

- **Turf Issues**—Smith felt that they operated too much in what he called "stovepipes" (territorial groups that saw themselves as internally competitive rather than mutually supportive). The old joke was Pennsylvania (Bell) would celebrate if New Jersey (Bell) lost a rate case—even though they were both a part of Bell Atlantic! In order to truly compete in a global economy, the new Bell Atlantic couldn't act as five separate state organizations or separate functional areas. They had to become a more unified, effective operation.

- **Bias for Action/Less Bureaucracy**—It was clear that no matter what shifts took place to improve the business, a greater sense of urgency was needed at all levels of the organization. Things had to be done faster, with fewer committees, fewer meetings, shorter reviews, lower-level sign-offs and fewer people in the decision cycle.

Smith had tried in his first year to change the culture. He gave many speeches and admonished his team on many occasions, but that wasn't enough to create a change. Bell Atlantic's experience was common to many organizations. Shifting organizational habits is not easy and merely talking or communicating about it doesn't work. People and organizations shift as a result of deeper insights that come from experience. Smith realized that in order for people to truly understand what he was saying, they had to experience it. Without that experience, the principles would remain abstract concepts.

He also knew that transformational change had to come from the top. So we developed an insight-based, offsite experiential workshop to give his senior team a shared experience of the new culture. The Bell Atlantic officers spent three days in an environment of increased accountability, trust, open communication, feedback, listening and teamwork. It was exactly the experience they needed. Just as it's impossible to really understand the culture of a foreign country from reading a book, it's hard for people to comprehend a new corporate culture just by talking or reading about it. They have to experience it.

After the retreat, many said "Ah-ha, now we understand what Ray has been talking about!" They made a gut-level commitment to new behaviors and created what they called The Bell Atlantic Way, which included the values, behaviors and philosophies they felt were the necessary foundations of the new culture. The Bell Atlantic Way became the guideline for conducting their business internally and externally. It was their code of conduct, a statement describing their new culture. They also decided they wanted all of the managers and supervisors under them to experience this new culture in teams just as they had. This led to a cultural transformation and to Bell Atlantic becoming an early leader and innovator in the phone industry. They moved from being five very separate and monopolistic state phone companies to national competitor in an acquisition mode.

NYNEX, another "Baby Bell" led by Bill Ferguson and Ivan Seidenberg (currently Verizon's Chairman and Chief Executive Officer), also recognized the need to shift their culture. They created a similar process with values and behaviors, not unlike Bell Atlantic's, which they took to all of their employees. They called their process "Winning Ways." Even during a period of dramatic downsizing and uncertainty at NYNEX, employee attitude actually improved, a phenomenon attributed to employees' engagement in Senn-Delaney Leadership's *Winning Ways* process.

Bell Atlantic and NYNEX merged companies and cultures, and after the Bell Atlantic-GTE merger, became Verizon. They continue to be an innovator in the field of telecommunications and while the future of that industry is uncertain, they appear well positioned from a cultural standpoint to continue to innovate and make the changes necessary to succeed.

Verizon serves as a perfect example of an organization that systematically aligned its strategy, structure and culture. They moved from a monopolistic to a competitive strategy, from a set of semi-autonomous, geographically-defined state phone companies to an integrated international company, and from a bureaucratic, entitlement culture to a more agile and accountable one. An important part of that effort was defining the culture they needed to best succeed in the new competitive market they were entering. To do that, they selected the The Bell Atlantic Way Behaviors that appear on the next page (Figure 7.5).[29]

THE BELL ATLANTIC WAY BEHAVIORS

Our Responsibilities:

As Bell Atlantic employees, we share the responsibility to fully support our company's vision and the goals and strategies that will take us there. Therefore we must

- **Team Play.** This means that I constantly ask the questions "Who is Bell Atlantic?" "What is my team's purpose, and does that meet the requirements of customers, employees, shareowners, or communities?" Also, I do not foster internal competition. I focus my energy on new ways to create a win for the entire team.
- **Accept Accountability.** This means asking, "What more can I do to get the results?" rather than looking for reasons why something did not get done. Accountable people look for ways to get the job done.
- **Empower.** I empower people when I trust them to do the job and do it well. I give them the authority and the resources they need to do their best, and I offer support and coaching to help them through.
- **Care About and Recognize Others**. This means I truly care about the personal and professional well-being of my colleagues, and I go out of my way to recognize their achievements and make them feel appreciated and valuable.
- **Listen and Be Here Now.** This means that when I am with someone, I care about what they have to say. I put other thoughts out of my mind so that I can "Be Here Now" with that person.
- **Encourage Risk.** I get outside the "9 Dots" (outside of my comfort zone) to solve a problem even if I am not sure what the results will be. I show the members of my team that the only way to lose is by not trying to win.
- **Focus on Priority Issues.** I prioritize my time so that I take care of my "blue chips" first. I trust other members of my team with those things I don't have time to take care of myself.

Figure 7.5 © 1992 Bell Atlantic Corporation. Used with Permission.

ALIGNING CULTURE WITH A SERVICE STRATEGY

Another example of a successful telecommunications company is T-Mobile. They are a well-known and highly respected brand, but one of the smaller players in a cellular market that has seen much consolidation. As such, they needed to find a competitive edge other than size.

T-Mobile's strategy is to provide the best value by being a lower-cost provider while delivering superior service and customer care. They did not want to be seen as just "cheaper," so they put great emphasis on creating a culture with personalized customer service. Their CEO, Robert Dotson, believed that brand awareness based on superior value and service would lead to greater customer loyalty and lower customer turnover, known in the cellular industry as "churn." He and his senior team rewrote the strategy and reshaped the organization's structure and systems to align with that strategy.

They also took time to engage in a culture-shaping process, which included defining a set of accountable, customer-focused, team-based behaviors called "Get more commitment." The transformational process was so successful that within 24 months T-Mobile moved from 7th place on the JD Powers customer ratings to No.1, and has held that position for several years. The shift in culture helped decrease their turnover, which significantly reduced costs and impacted the bottom line.

T-Mobile is a great example of how culture can support strategy and create a competitive advantage.

Culture and Organizational Model

Insurance is another traditional industry that has faced change in the recent past. Nationwide's CEO wanted to change their organizational model from a holding company to a shared business model (structure). He believed that by doing so he could gain the synergies available from their three separate business units to working closer together. This dictated that Nationwide's cultural definition needed to place great emphasis on teamwork, cross-organizational collaboration and decisions for the greater good. Shifting the culture has allowed the 100-year-old company to move from a holding corporation to a shared business model in a short period of time and dramatically improve profits.

ACTION STEPS

If your organization is implementing a new strategy or shifting the structure, ask the following questions:

1. What habits in our culture will get in the way of this change or slow it down?

   Depts - us vs them

   even w/in depts - turf, entitlement

2. What qualities do we need to add or strengthen in our culture?

   Flexibility

   trust

   Respect

3. Do we have the necessary alignment between our strategy, our structure and the behavioral traits to execute? If implementing changes or creating results seems difficult, chances are these elements are not aligned.

   _No_

4. What cultural shifts are needed to align them?

The process for *defining* the needed culture is covered in the next chapter.

8

THE ROAD MAP TO SUCCESS: DEFINING VALUES IN THE DESIRED CULTURE

"If you don't know where you are going, any road will get you there."

—*Lewis Carroll*

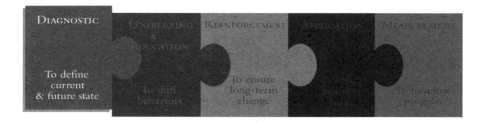

Figure 8.1 © 2006 Senn-Delaney Leadership Consulting Group, LLC.

From the standpoint of culture shaping, one rule is, "if you can't define it, you can't create it." So, the second part of the **D** in the DURAM™ culture-shaping model is **Define**. The definition usually takes the form of an organization's values and guiding behaviors. These are "the rules of road" for the behavior of every individual in an organization. They also provide a template for all HR reinforcement systems.

In their book, *Corporate Culture and Performance*, John P. Kotter and James L. Heskett document the connection between strong cultures and exceptional results. After following a number of companies over a ten-year period, they concluded that organizations that better lived their value statements were more effective, because their managers and leaders consistently exhibited the behaviors needed to win.[30]

Shared values create a template for both corporate and individual behavior. When these values are clearly stated and accepted by all members of the organization, they set guidelines and standards for making decisions, determining priorities, solving problems and addressing competitive pressures.

A High-Performance Culture

"Our job is to provide a culture in which people can flourish and reach their dreams—in which they can be all they want to be."

—*Jack Welch*[31]
Former chairman of GE

No two cultures are exactly the same. And, just as there is no one perfect personality, there is no one perfect culture. However, organizations that possess a healthy, high-performance culture all have a similar feeling about them. Over the years, Senn-Delaney Leadership has asked senior executives at our retreats to describe their idea of a high-performance organizational culture. Remarkably, they all expressed similar feelings and even used many of the same words. Typical descriptions include:

"It would be a flexible and highly adaptive culture where employees display a 'can-do' attitude, a contagious sense of optimism and belief in themselves and our products and services. People at all levels would feel energized, motivated and would be growing both personally and professionally by being a part of the company."

"A high-performance culture maintains a healthy perspective and balance between numbers/results and people/relationships. It is a place with high integrity where everyone understands where the company wants to go, has a focus on the customer, knows what is important and everyone is part of a winning team."

One manager in our process described it this way:

"There's lightness as well as a winning spirit here that makes our workloads seem energizing and rarely stressful and tiresome!"

Sound ideal?

Sound impossible?

Worth having?

You Bet!

High-performance organizations do exist, but they don't happen by accident, or without senior leaders who value their organizational culture and are willing to work at it. In our interviews for the book *21st Century Leadership*, we interviewed 100 top leaders. The kinds of winning shared values they mentioned include:

- Integrity and honesty

- Empowering leadership

- Openness and trust

- Teamwork and mutual support

- Caring

- Openness to change

- Quality, service and a customer focus

- Respect for the individual and for diversity

- Winning and being the best

- Innovation

- Personal accountability

- A can-do attitude

- Balance in life

- Positive attitude and optimism

On the next page (Figure 8.2) is a list of distinctions between cultural barriers and winning behaviors.

CULTURAL BARRIERS VERSUS WINNING BEHAVIORS

Cultural Barriers	Winning Behaviors
• Hierarchical leadership—boss driven	• Empowering leadership
• Turf issues	• Teamwork and mutual support
• Opportunism and lack of principles	• Ethics and integrity
• Hidden agendas, lack of openness and passive aggressive behaviors	• Open, honest and flowing communications, and a willingness to confront issues
• Distrust and fear	• Trust
• Short-term focus; strictly bottom-line driven	• Profit-focus with an eye to long-term organizational health and customer service
• Task-orientation and internal focus	• Customer/market-orientation and external focus
• "Can't be done" attitude	• "Can-do" spirit
• Blame and making excuses	• Personal responsibility and accountability
• Codependence and excessive independence	• Interdependence
• Prejudice and judgment	• Diversity, respect for differences and curiosity
• Little or no training	• Continuous learning and knowledge development
• Stress and burnout	• Focus and balance
• Holding onto the past and resisting change	• Innovation, ingenuity and breakthroughs
• Strict rules and rigid policies	• Flexible, fluid, and rapidly responsive
• Win/lose games	• Win/win games and bigger wins for entire organization
• Command and control	• Coaching—appreciative and constructive feedback

Figure 8.2 © 2006 Senn-Delaney Leadership Consulting Group, LLC.

SIX ESSENTIAL VALUES

We have concluded that there are definable Essential Values that are lived by those organizations, teams and leaders that are consistently winners. It seems that there is a universal set of principles of life effectiveness governing both performance and quality of life. Dr. Abraham Maslow's early work in the 1950's on the theory of human motivation—known as Maslow's Hierarchy of Needs, supports the existence of these inner, natural life-effectiveness principles. These principles help to explain:

- Why some companies more consistently perform well while others don't.

- What makes a company a great place to work.

- Why great business teams, like sports teams, are more than the sum of their parts, while so many others are dysfunctional.

- Why some individuals consistently do well in their careers and personal lives while other very talented individuals struggle.

Healthy, high-performance values and behaviors exist in all of us when we are at our best. Some people are simply able to exhibit them more consistently than others. You have undoubtedly experienced times when ideas just flowed and relationships worked easily. These were times you felt most capable and at the top of your game. High-performance, life-enhancing behaviors are available to each of us when we are operating at the top of our game. They also emerge naturally and more often for people who are immersed in a healthy culture.

To make this concept more real and personal, we have asked hundreds of leaders to make a list of the values, traits or characteristics in themselves that they believe created the results and fulfillment they have experienced in their lives. When we consolidate these lists, they always contain some form of the descriptions of the categories we call the *Essential Value Set*. When we ask teams to describe what it's like when they are operating at the top of their game, they come up with comparable lists.

What is the *Essential Value Set*? It includes:

- A *performance value*, with an emphasis on personal accountability and a focus on achieving results

- A *collaborative value* in the form of teamwork, healthy relationships and mutual support

- A *change value* exhibited by openness to change, innovation and commitment to growth and learning

- An *individual/organizational emotional health value* represented by trust, respect, positive energy, and a more hopeful, optimistic attitude

- A *foundational integrity and ethics value*, consisting of honesty, truthfulness, fairness and social responsibility, that is used to guide daily decisions and behavior

- A *service or purpose value*, such as making a difference for others, including customers

We refer to this as a set because it is an interconnected and mutually supporting group of values and behaviors. All need to be present in sufficient strength to create the positive outcomes in our life. In fact, when we find an individual, team or organization that is very strong in one value and yet very weak in another, we can accurately predict the dysfunctions that exist and the difficulties they will encounter.

Let's explore further what each value represents.

The Performance Value

This might be called the "make it happen" value because little happens in life without action. It is described in different ways by different people as performance orientation, high standards, high expectations, a bias for action, resourcefulness, proactiveness or just plain hard work. The essence of this value is a belief in personal accountability and ownership of results. It is the exact opposite of a "victim mindset," because whenever we exhibit victim tendencies, we are blaming other people or events for our lack of results. We make excuses, rationalize or "live in hope" that something will happen.

An accountability mindset is the opposite of the victim mindset. Organizations lacking accountability often have an entitlement mindset vs. a performance mindset. Too much time and effort is spent on explaining why numbers are missed and why "it's not my fault." Pay for tenure vs. pay for performance is a part of this dysfunctional entitlement culture.

Leaders who embrace accountability focus their energy on taking appropriate action steps; they are oriented more to the future than the past. They ask themselves, "What more can I do to get results in spite of obstacles?"

While most leaders consider themselves to be, and for the most part are, very accountable, constant vigilance is necessary because even successful people, especially those who like to be right, can easily fall into "it's not my fault habit." This then sanctions that behavior in the organization. Leaders often fall short in holding their own people accountable by casting a shadow of blaming other departments, outside competitors or circumstances. We find leaders and organizations with strong performance values constantly ask, "What more can we or you do to get the desired results?"

"Don't Blame Me!"

How many times have you heard people say, "Don't Blame Me!"? In his book, *A Nation of Victims*, Charles J. Sykes points to the decline in American competitiveness and the erosion in our quality of life as being linked to a general feeling of lack of control, a sense of having no power over events or circumstances. Sykes calls this as "the victimization of America." He references a series of magazine articles that highlight this sense of victimization:

- *New York Magazine*—"The New Culture of Victimization—Don't Blame Me!"

- *Time*—"Crybabies: Eternal Victims"

- *Esquire*—"A Confederacy of Complainers"

- *Harpers*—"Victims All?"[32]

Victim attitudes subtly abound in organizations: blaming, excuses, "CYA" activities, "it's not my job," "they did it," etc. There are hundreds of behaviors and attitudes that people use as a shield against taking risks and being personally accountable. These negative attitudes directly impact productivity, efficiency and the bottom line.

When attitudes of personal accountability are dominant in organizations, more of the vital work gets done. Individuals and teams overcome seemingly impossible obstacles when they have a high sense of personal and organizational accountability—the belief that our own actions or inactions are the major cause of success or failure. Accountable people believe they have a great deal of control over their destiny and use their ability to make choices as their greatest tool to influence outcomes and create results.

> *"It's choice, not chance, that determines your destiny."*
> —*Jean Nidetch*
> *Weight Watchers founder*

We can enhance our personal and organizational accountability, while shedding non-productive victim attitudes, by increasing our awareness of accountability and using our ability to choose the attitudes that are most constructive. When we do this, we look for the productive options present in every situation. In addition, when a situation doesn't go well, we can ask accountable questions like:

- What clues did I ignore?

- What extra steps could I have taken?

- What actions did I avoid?

- What should I have known?

- Whom should I have confronted sooner?

- What personality traits or habits of mine might have aggravated this situation?

- Once I handle this, how can I avoid it in the future?

Here's an important caveat: *Never use the practice of personal accountability as a hammer on yourself or others.* Remember, it is not possible to be 100 percent accountable for everything all of the time. Expecting such accountability from yourself or employees is not realistic and often creates negative feelings that can cause both results and organizational climate to suffer.

One CEO we worked with became so excited about the accountability concept that he put a sign on a stick—a paddle—that said, "VICTIM." If anyone got out of line in a meeting, he would hold up the paddle and give everyone a lecture. You can guess what happened. People just shut up in meetings and complained in the halls afterward about how he had "victimized" them. With coaching, he gave up the paddle and found more constructive ways to create accountability, because the most effective way to make the point was for him to behave in a more accountable fashion and not "blame" his team through the use of his paddle. Afterwards, when excuses for non-performance came up in meetings, he would merely ask the question, with true curiosity, "Are there any ideas on what more we can do given the situation?" That led to much more accountable discussions and action plans.

ENERGY LOSS ON "WHAT IS"

One of the greatest energy drains in an organization is the time wasted complaining about things that no amount of action is likely to change. These circumstances could be referred to as "what is." Obvious candidates are the fact that:

- We do have competition.

- There is a corporate or parent organization.

- We do have a boss.

- We do have tight budgets.

- We do get older and pay taxes.

- Weather and traffic are bad sometimes.

- The economy, interest rates and other things do fluctuate.

It amazes us how much time and energy people spend talking about the specific "what is" issues in a company. If you listen carefully, you will hear what they are in your firm.

This raises the question, "How can I be sure I am using my energy well, and not overdoing accountability and burning myself out?" We see two answers to that one.

First, ask the question, "What more can I reasonably do, in spite of any obstacles that exist?" That will move you back to action, if action steps are available.

Since accountable people can always see more that could be done, where do you draw the line? The second answer to this seemingly endless pursuit of perfection and the problem of the "what is" lies in the Serenity Prayer attributed to American theologian Reinhold Niebuhr:

"Grant me the serenity to accept the things I cannot change,

the courage to change the things I can,

and the wisdom to know the difference."

The Collaborative Value

Having a performance value alone is not enough, because leadership takes place in the context of a team. In today's complex, interconnected world, major accomplishments are rarely due to one individual. The strength of the team has become more important than the strength of the individual, hence there are very few "individual star systems" left in business or team sports.

Collaboration is people playing win-win versus win-lose games and being willing to make decisions for the greater good versus self-interest. In fact, one way to define a healthy, high-performance culture is:

A collection of healthy, high-performance teams working together for the greater good.

The collaborative value is often simply described as *teamwork* and *mutual support*. While this is true, it is more than that. A team at Pacific Gas and Electric, a large California power utility company, spent many hours wrestling with this value as they worked on their cultural definitions. They initially considered using the word *teamwork* to describe this characteristic but decided not to. They already had excellent teamwork *within* many individual teams. What they, like many companies, needed was better cross-organizational collaboration *between* teams to tackle complex issues like business transformation. They choose to use the word *collaboration* for that very reason.

We all know how much teams working at their best can accomplish. Unfortunately, enormous energy is lost in most organizations from we-they finger-pointing issues, turf battles and divisions operating in structural silos. Just imagine how much more successful your organization could be if all that wasted energy was focused on getting a common result. That's why good leaders know it's worth their time and effort to build great teams and make sure the teams are connected for the common good.

"When teamwork kicks in, nobody can beat you."

—Don Shula
Head Coach, Miami Dolphins
(the only NFL team to attain a perfect 17–0 season)

Today's complex business environment requires a high degree of *interdependence* within organizations. Implementing changes and serving customers requires people to work together in new ways. In a high-performance culture, collaboration replaces individualism and competition between departments. The essence of collaboration is the belief that "we all belong to the same team and must work together to achieve the overall goals. I don't succeed unless and until the entire team succeeds."

Poor organizational collaboration can be extremely expensive. We have seen huge investments in major business transformation projects wasted because business units and functions wouldn't sacrifice self-interest for the greater good. We have also seen competing internal groups spend millions of dollars of their own time, and that of their external consultants', trying to prove another division or function wrong. Extreme competitiveness between department or divisional teams can take the form of withholding critical information from a competing group, regardless of the damage to the entire organization.

Jon Katzenbach, formerly of McKinsey & Company and co-author of *The Wisdom of Teams*, speaks about teamwork with true passion. When asked why team training is so popular, his reply was:

> *"Because good teams produce extra performance results. There is virtually no environment in which teams—if done right—can't have a measurable impact on the performance of an organization."*[33]

While these benefits are critical to the success of an organization, there is also a set of human benefits from teamwork that greatly enhance the working environment and create a terrific place to work:

- Teamwork fills the human desire for socialization and self-esteem through recognition by others.

- The need to learn and grow is best fulfilled in a team environment.

- Working together for a common goal is motivating and provides a sense of purpose and fulfillment.

The Change Value

Innovation and agility are two qualities organizations are seeking today. Healthy individuals, teams and organizations need to continually learn and grow because their success is closely tied to their agility and responsiveness. Agile organizations are more fluid and less bureaucratic because they are governed by values and guiding behaviors rather than policies and procedures.

Organizations that score low in the change value tend to have what we call an observer/critic mindset. Leaders in those organizations tend to see why new ideas won't work, as opposed to determining how to make them work. Individuals that do well at change are resourceful and innovative when it comes to ideas and open to feedback and coaching when it comes to personal growth.

Change leadership involves four dimensions:

1. **Being open to continuous self-examination, introspection and change.** One large corporation we studied was headed by a leader who talked almost exclusively about the past—the "good old days." In this and other ways he signaled that he had stopped growing, and the organization was feeling the effects. People who embrace change recognize that reaching one's potential as a leader or a person is a lifelong journey—not a destination.

2. **The ability to be an effective change agent.** This means learning to introduce change and lead change. In today's fast-moving business world, a change agent is someone who invites and fuels innovation and continually looks for ways to improve everything. As Jack Welch said, as part of GE's values[34], you need to *relish* change, not just accept it.

3. **Seeing possibilities in new ideas.** One of the traditional beliefs about being a leader is, "If I'm shown a new idea, my job is to figure out what's wrong with it." This is what we learned and practiced in "management by exception." We were taught to be observer/critics: people who challenge new ideas, play the devil's advocate, and try to find inconsistencies. In this new era of change, cultures and people need to live in a constant state of curiosity and exploration, rather than criticism and excessive judgment.

4. **Coaching and feedback.** If you want to change behaviors in an organization, you need a feedback-rich environment. Unfortunately, this is the cultural trait that usually rates lowest in Senn-Delaney Leadership's cultural profile diagnostic tool. Four embedded beliefs get in the way:

- "People at this level shouldn't need my coaching."

- "Saying nice things to people (appreciating them) is too 'soft' a thing to do and they will slack off."

- "I don't want to make them or myself uncomfortable."

- "I don't have the time."

- "I don't feel comfortable giving constructive feedback."

All of these beliefs get in the way of coaching and feedback. In reality, it doesn't take long to say "thank you," and everyone has areas for improvement and needs coaching. Done right, coaching strengthens people and relationships.

What do we mean by "done right"?

- Coach someone when you or they are higher on the Mood Elevator. They'll be less defensive and have ears to hear it.

- Provide more appreciative feedback at work and at home.

- Come from a mindset of being supportive. For example, "I see areas where you could be even more effective."

Expressing appreciation is one of the simplest and least expensive ways of motivating and rewarding people. Saying thank you, adding positive comments to emails and celebrating outstanding efforts are simple, cost-effective ways to let people know they are appreciated and valued.

Additionally, providing constructive feedback on how to improve performance is as important as expressing appreciation for work well done. All employees want to know how to do their jobs better. Most employees feel they do not receive enough coaching and feedback. Because they don't know how they're doing, they don't know what to change in order to improve.

High-performance organizations encourage people to expand their knowledge, increase their productivity and reach their potential. A healthy, growth-oriented work environment is one that is coaching and feedback-rich. It provides the information people need to continuously improve their performance. In this environment, employees see coaching as an important part of their job descriptions. The coach helps people become winners by reaching their peak performance.

The Personal/Organizational Health Value

Most people believe that ethics or integrity is the foundational value. We agree, but believe there is another foundational value that is just as important, but not as well understood or utilized in most organizations. That value is a healthy state of mind characterized by openness, trust and respect. The following traits are a part of individuals, teams and organizations with healthier states of mind. They:

- Are more hopeful and optimistic

- Generate far more positive than negative energy

- Assume best intentions versus negative motives in others

- Tend to be more present and listen more openly to others' points of view

- Operate in the higher states of the Mood Elevator with curiosity and encouragement

- Have higher emotional intelligence

- Maintain their perspective and their bearings better in challenging situations

The value of these qualities is often underestimated, even though they are the qualities that make a company great, for employees, customers and shareholders. They are indicators that people are operating "at their best." The key premise is that this healthy state of mind is a natural state in all of us. It is not dictated by outside events or influences, but rather is an optimistic belief in ourselves and others on our teams.

Health as described here provides the strongest foundation because all of the other values come naturally in abundance when people are operating in their healthiest state. One of the reasons healthy state of mind adds to business results is that it is synonymous with higher "emotional intelligence." The research by Daniel Goleman in his book, *Emotional Intelligence: Why It Can Matter More Than IQ,* has provided proof that people with high "EQ" do better in life and make better leaders.

Ethics and Integrity

Ethics and integrity are considered a foundational value in most every organization. In fact, when you speak to most people about values, they often think exclusively about things like integrity and respect, as compared to the broader Essential Value Set. A good example of too narrow a definition of values is a conversation we had with a CEO who said, "We've got great values and we live them—but we do have some issues like passive/aggressive behaviors, turf issues and trust."

Ethics and integrity are cornerstones of all high-performance cultures. The word "integrity" implies consistency or congruence between words and deeds, while "ethics" suggests a system of moral standards that an organization or individual uses to guide decisions and daily behaviors. The most common elements of ethics and integrity are: honesty, truthfulness, fairness and social responsibility. For individuals, they are rooted in beliefs like "my word is my bond."

Most of the massive corporate failures in the early 2000's were due to breaches in the ethics and integrity value. These failures underline the importance of not taking ethics and integrity for granted, and remaining insistent that they are an essential foundation of the organization. There is a need to refocus on ethics to reestablish trust, not only with the public, but with employees.

The integrity value is vital to the obligations of leadership because it goes directly to the matter of whether leaders are really "walking the talk." It is a cornerstone of culture shaping because early on in the process, the big question on people's minds is, "Are the top leaders living the values?"

The Service or Purpose Value

"Why are we in business? What is our purpose as a firm?" This question is often answered in a company's vision or mission statement. For many companies, including Senn-Delaney Leadership, this is how and where the purpose value is addressed. Others feel customers are so important that they also need to be a part of the stated values or rules of the road for behaviors. An important distinction here is that the Service or Purpose Value reaches beyond just superior customer service, and actually looks to impact or improve the customer's experience in life. This value is most prevalent when a team or organization is working for a purpose beyond themselves and they are focused on "Making a Difference." When an organization is focused on this broader purpose, it will tap into Maslow's hierarchical needs for personal and organizational self-actualization. This means becoming everything one is capable of becoming.

The value statement can take different forms. For example:

■ Making a Difference in Our Customers' Lives or

■ Building a Better Future Together

The service or purpose value helps bring meaning to the job. It also focuses people on customers as the lifeblood of the organization and reason for its existence.

Adding Meaning to Core Values: Defining Guiding Behaviors

A professed value such as collaboration is not specific enough to guide and align people's behaviors. To some it might mean being a good team player in their department, to others it might mean being a team contributor to the broader organization. Personal accountability to one person might mean doing their own job well and no more, while to another it might mean being accountable for the success of teammates or looking for any way they can contribute to the overall success of the organization.

Senn-Delaney Leadership is often asked to look at why culture-shaping initiatives are not working, even though a company may have written values. We find that there are a wide variety of interpretations of what those values mean. We have concluded that it's critical in the culture-shaping process to very explicitly define each core value with a set of guiding behaviors that clearly explain the meaning of that value.

Here's an example of the way we define teamwork via guiding behaviors:

SENN-DELANEY LEADERSHIP TEAMWORK VALUE & GUIDING BEHAVIORS

We partner with our clients and with each other.

1. Values, respects and is open to the points of view of others and seeks the wisdom of the team to meet Senn-Delaney and client needs
2. Seeks to understand client needs and partners to provide satisfying solutions to those needs
3. Is unselfish in seeking the best outcomes rather than those that benefit him/her most
4. Partners by developing open, trusting, respectful working relationships and a team spirit with clients and teammates
5. Takes responsibility for bringing other people and resources into the process in order to achieve a broader win
6. Contributes to effective working relationships and teamwork within and across organizational boundaries

---

Figure 8.3 © 2006 Senn-Delaney Leadership Consulting Group, LLC.

As you can see, collaboration and teamwork go beyond being willing to cooperate. In our definition, it requires someone to not be territorial but, in addition, be willing to sacrifice individual or departmental goals in order to accomplish a bigger win for the client and overall organization.

Guiding behaviors also allow a company to much more specifically define the unique differences and priorities in their own culture. They also provide flexibility in terms of how many categories of values are needed. For example, respect for individuals could be a guiding behavior under teamwork, and creative thinking or innovation could be a guiding behavior under embracing change.

Guiding behaviors fill another need for organizations: they provide a specific list of observable behaviors that can become the foundation of human resources reinforcement systems including selection, orientation, performance management, succession planning and 360° feedback (as described in Chapter 15).

A Process to Discover and Develop Your Own High-Performance Culture

"Values come from the heart, not the head."

We have developed processes that help leaders identify their organization's most empowering vision, values and winning behaviors. The approach is based on the fact that vision and values need to come from the heart and not just the head. One common error in defining shared values is making it an intellectual exercise or series of discussions. Values must come from deeply-held beliefs about how leaders want their employees and company to operate. It is what is valued, and held important by those leaders, that makes the difference in a healthy, high-performing organization.

A second error in writing statements of values and guiding behaviors is doing it in a paternalistic way. Guiding behaviors should be written so that each and every employee in the organization can own them. Statements like, "We will develop our people" perpetuates dependence and hierarchy. A more appropriate statement is, "We are all committed to continuous personal and professional growth."

One way to avoid these errors is to create a process that is experiential, not intellectual. We use a custom-designed Leadership and Culture Shaping offsite retreat. The senior team usually goes to an off-site location with few business agendas and distractions. There, leadership and teambuilding activities with customized experiential exercises enable the senior team to experience the essential values as well as more productive ways of working together on issues. By *experiencing* a more open, trusting environment, better team interaction and more supportive coaching and feedback, the senior team connects to the kind of culture they want for their organization and for themselves at an emotional *and* intellectual level. They also come to understand the power of their state of mind and moods on their leadership.

This kind of setting is most conducive to identifying the vision and values that touch and move people. Visions and values cannot be developed through a logical, analytical process alone. When people connect to their values very personally, they are also more willing to commit to living them.

Action Steps

As you reflect on this chapter, you might ask yourself the following questions:

1. Which of the essential values (performance, collaboration...) do I live best and which should I work on personally?

   _____

   _____

2. Which of the essential values does my organization or team excel at and where do we come up short?

   _____

   _____

3. Do we have the appropriate values to shape our culture or should we revisit them?

   _____

   _____

4. Are our values hanging on the wall and are they alive and in action in the halls?

   _____

   _____

5. Do we have the guiding behaviors needed to bring meaning to the values, or are they buried somewhere in our competency model or elsewhere?

   _____

   _____

9

THE HUMAN OPERATING SYSTEM

Most people would agree that essential high-performance values like personal accountability, collaboration and innovation contribute to winning teams and winning cultures. What is not as obvious is that we live those values automatically when we are at our best, operating higher on the Mood Elevator. So why don't leaders and teams live them more consistently? We believe the answer can be found in achieving a better understanding of what drives our behaviors and at times prevents us from being at our best.

An understanding of the **Human Operating System** provides insight into what makes each of us "tick." It answers some interesting "whys":

- Why we behave as we do

- Why we are so effective sometimes and ineffective other times

- Why others behave in ways that don't make sense to us

- Why we see the world and others the way we do

- Why others often see things differently than we do

- Why we feel the way we do

- Why we live the essential values sometimes and not all the time

The *Human Operating System* is a phrase first suggested to us by the former CEO of Compaq Computer. During a culture-shaping process we conducted with his senior team, he explained that computers can only communicate with each other if they share a common *operating system*. His insight was that our process was teaching him and his team the human operating system that would enable them to work better together and understand why they each behaved the way they did.

There are four foundational principles in the Human Operating System (HOS):

HOS Principle #1 — Managing Energy is a key to healthy, high-performance

Are there some days you have plenty of energy to take on the challenges of the world and others where you feel overwhelmed and de-energized? Are there ever times you felt tired and in a low mood at the end of a day but felt re-energized the next day after a good night's sleep?

Energy exists in many forms around us. Meetings can be energizing or draining, just as people can be.

> LARRY: I am keenly aware that some people I know or interact with are "energy pumps" and others can be "energy drains." I prefer to fill my world with partners and teammates that know how to create, direct and preserve energy.

Jim Loehr, co-author of the book *The Power of Full Engagement* (New York: Free Press, a division of Simon and Schuster, Inc. 2003), has made a career of working with peak athletes and trying to translate their success to executives. The subtitle of his book and conclusion of his work is:

Managing Energy, Not Time, is the Key to High Performance and Personal Renewal

ORGANIZATIONAL ENERGY

As analysts of culture, it is easy for us to notice different kinds of energy as we visit companies and observe teams. We see some that have a healthy, high pace and others that are just plain stressed. This is usually confirmed by one of our diagnostics tools. One of the questions on our team and culture profile instrument (page 21) measures this aspect of human energy as it exists in organizations and teams. At one end of the seven-point scale is the phrase "healthy/fast paced environment." At the other end of the scale is "high stress/burn-out pace." Most people like to work in dynamic, energizing, fast paced environments. It can be stimulating, motivating, and produce great results. As the pace ramps up and the psychological rewards like feeling valued and connected to a purpose decrease, the healthy, fast-paced environment begins to feel stressful. In recent years, as we first met clients, we found more and more of them "in the red," with scores in the high stress/burn-out zone on their culture profile.

Many people are beginning to feel overwhelmed by the amount of work they have to do, the number of meetings they have to attend, and the number of emails or BlackBerry messages they scramble to respond to. As their stress score drops into the red, they descend down on the Mood Elevator and their creativity and effectiveness drop as well. The constant distractions erode people's ability to be fully present for others, and the quality of their relationships decrease, both at work and at home.

Positive/productive energy comes in different forms. High positive energy includes enthusiasm, determination and commitment. Less intense, quieter positive energy includes creativity, trust, listening and optimism. Spending more time in these states of mind contributes to more fulfilling and productive lives, teams and organizations. That is why energy is a key principle in the Human Operating System; to the degree that we recognize its value, we gain the ability to manage our energy, and therefore our lives, even more effectively.

HOS Principle #2 — Our thinking drives our behaviors

One of the most common "dysfunctions" we see in organizations is the existence of turf issues and lack of cross-organizational teamwork. Even though there may be only one stock price for a company, often different groups, functions or business units behave in ways that reduce overall corporate results. This is especially true if, by doing so, they can look better or gain an advantage. What drives a behavior that consistently reduces results?

The answer can be seen in one of the exercises Senn-Delaney Leadership uses to make the point in our workshops. We put people in pairs and give them a time limit in which to "score points." In most cases, they assume that their job is to beat the other person and score more points themselves at the expense of their partner. If we have multiple pairs in the room, each pair will assume that they have to beat the other pairs. If we divide the room into two groups, one group will assume that they have to beat the second group. Interestingly, beating the other person or group is not at all part of the instructions and not, in fact, how the game is won, yet nearly everyone assumes that this is the objective.

What is the root of this strong habit in individuals and teams? It has to do with our programming. Most of us grow up taking part in games where there is a winner and a loser. These life experiences, combined with our high internal drive for results, lead to the belief that, "for me to win, someone else has to lose." Over time, this belief becomes an unconscious habit that drives our behaviors, often at the expense of results and relationships.

For me to win, someone else has to lose!

Unfortunately, in most organizations, more time and energy is spent on internal competition than on meeting competitive threats from the outside. This unconscious win/lose behavior shows up at home and work in everyday interactions such as arguing with a loved one and having to be right about something of absolutely no consequence.

When it comes to win-lose behaviors, it could be said that people are just doing what makes sense to them based on their thinking, even though it may be wrong at times—because their thinking is invisible to them (and to us)!

The connection between thinking, behaviors and results is illustrated in the figure below which shows how "win-lose" thinking drives "lose-lose" behaviors.

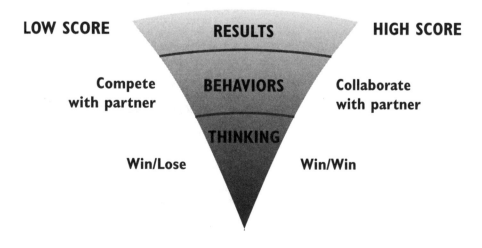

Figure 9.1 © 2006 Senn-Delaney Leadership Consulting Group, LLC.

In the "scoring points" exercise people see the objective through their own filters, including the thought habit, "For me to win, someone has to lose." Since our thought habits largely determine our behaviors, and our behaviors determine our results, the win-lose belief leads to misplaced competitiveness and a loss of results.

The Results Cone on the previous page illustrates the impact of just one thought habit, the win-lose thought habit. In reality, we each have dozens of thought habits, collected from the time we were children. Common thought habits include: "Big boys don't cry," "Clean your plate," and "If you can't say something nice, don't say anything at all." In adulthood, these beliefs can lead to dysfunctional behaviors like suppressing emotions, overeating and avoidance of confronting others about their negative behaviors. Consequences can include health problems, unsatisfying relationships and poor results.

Many of our thought habits affect our leadership and life effectiveness. See if any of these sound familiar:

- I'm the boss; I'm not supposed to make mistakes. (So I make excuses.)

- It doesn't pay to take any risks around here. (So I won't take a chance and innovate.)

- Don't contradict a peer in a meeting. (So I talk about it in the hallway afterwards.)

- I don't have time to coach. (So my people get no development.)

- It's better to play it safe. (So I'm risk-averse and change-averse.)

- True professionals don't need appreciative feedback. (So employees feel unappreciated and are less engaged.)

- If others look good it takes away from me. (So I don't support others and instead put them down.)

- It's best to avoid conflict and be polite. (So I substitute passive-aggressive behaviors.)

- If you want a job done right, you have to do it yourself. (So I don't delegate enough.)

Organizations, like people, develop collective thought habits that define their culture. When turf issues and "we-they" behaviors exist, it is simply win-lose thinking in action.

We encounter many limiting beliefs that drive our behaviors and create cultural barriers. Here are some examples:

Limiting Beliefs

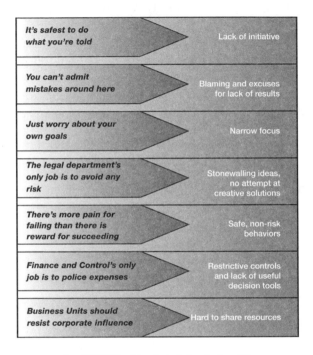

It's safest to do what you're told	Lack of initiative
You can't admit mistakes around here	Blaming and excuses for lack of results
Just worry about your own goals	Narrow focus
The legal department's only job is to avoid any risk	Stonewalling ideas, no attempt at creative solutions
There's more pain for failing than there is reward for succeeding	Safe, non-risk behaviors
Finance and Control's only job is to police expenses	Restrictive controls and lack of useful decision tools
Business Units should resist corporate influence	Hard to share resources

Figure 9.2 © 2006 Senn-Delaney Leadership Consulting Group, LLC.

There is value in understanding this aspect of what makes us "tick." It explains why external stimuli, like communication programs alone, are not successful in modifying behaviors. If our thinking about something is misguided, then our internal compass steers us astray. If we can create a change in our thinking, then a change in our behaviors will follow. As we gain a deeper appreciation for our own thought habits, we can more effectively monitor our behaviors. For example, if we catch ourselves with an unconstructive thought or behavior—such as win-lose competition—we can say to ourselves, "There I go again," or "Lets look for a bigger win," rather than acting on the old thought pattern.

Changes in thinking usually come as a result of insights or "ah-ha" moments. The new thinking creates a shift in a whole host of behaviors.

Change your thinking, change your behavior, change your life.

This concept can help us become better leaders, better team players and have more fulfilling relationships. It helps us deal with others better because when we truly understand that other people's behavior makes sense to them based on their thinking, we are less likely to take things personally. As a result, we can be less judgmental and more understanding. That doesn't mean we ignore inappropriate behavior. Our new understanding allows us to keep our own mental traction and handle situations better because we are less likely to lose our own mental bearings.

Our moment-to-moment behaviors are affected not only by the content of our thinking but the quality of our thinking. This is the essence of the third principle in the Human Operating System:

HOS Principle #3 — Our state of mind (quality of thinking) determines our effectiveness and quality of life

The third principle in the Human Operating System takes us back to the Mood Elevator in Chapter 2. In the second principle we talked about the content of our thinking—what we think—and how that drives our behaviors. The third principle has to do with what is best described as the nature or quality of our thinking. Unnecessary worry is an example of lower-quality thinking.

The quality of our thinking is what creates our state of mind or mood. When we are in a low mood, we often experience lower-quality thinking. In a state of irritation, worry or judgment, we don't lead as well, collaborate as well, coach as well or feel as good. Our higher moods, which come from higher-quality thinking, provide us greater insight, clarity and perspective. We are more resourceful and optimistic; we lead better, team better, coach better and feel better.

Our mood or state of mind is the most powerful filter through which we see the world. Our mood determines our quality of life and our moment-to-moment effectiveness. It also impacts everyone around us by casting a strong "shadow."

One of our clients had legendary mood swings. It was great to have a meeting with him when he was in the higher states; he had a terrific sense of humor, was open to ideas, listened well, and was collaborative and very creative. However, if you'd catch him on the wrong day, it was a different story. He was impatient, a poor listener, inflexible, judgmental and at times just plain rude. People constantly asked his executive assistant questions like "How is he today?" The insightful assistant finally devised a system to let people know whether it was a good day to talk to him. She would place one of two figurines on her desk in front of his office; a smiling figurine for a good day, and a frowning one for the bad days.

While this is a humorous anecdote, it resonates with too many people. It underscores the impact leaders can have on others by the mood they bring to work with them each day. Since leaders cast shadows that shape cultures, one shadow to be constantly aware of is the shadow cast by your mood. Never underestimate how well people are tuned in to your mood.

Our mood affects our own life as well as the lives of others. Your own state of mind will influence how you experience the world and how you behave. Understanding that is a critical step in creating the life you want and in helping create a healthy, high-performance culture.

Taking personal accountability for our state of mind is the highest form of accountability. That is made more difficult because we tend to believe that our mood is determined by our circumstances. However, the outside world or circumstances don't create our moods; rather, everyone has a choice about how they react to the world around them. So don't blame the world or situations for your mood. It is what you make of circumstances—your own thinking—that determines your mood. At a minimum, know that your thinking is less reliable in low mood states, so approach decision-making cautiously and act accordingly.

Most people take their moods as a given and don't feel accountable for managing them or adjusting for them. When individuals and teams better understand this concept and work together more often in their higher states, results are multiplied and stress is minimized.

Why do capable, well-intentioned people butt heads?

In Chapter 4 we talked about some common dysfunctions of teams. Why is it that bright, capable people can get so sideways with one another so easily? The answer lies in the fourth principle in the Human Operating System:

HOS Principle #4 — We each see the world through our own unique filters

The fourth principle in the Human Operating System helps explain why we have conflicts and disagreements with others. It also explains what we need to understand to contribute to more creative, effective meetings and have more respectful and loving relationships.

It's all based on the fact that we each see the world through our own unique set of filters. As a result, it might be said that we all live in a world of separate realities. Your reality is not my reality—and we both probably think we are right.

Look at the figure below. What first pops out for you?

Figure 9.3

For most people the face with the large nose is most obvious. But can you see the woman with sunglasses cradling the baby in her arm? If you can't and need a clue, his nose is her flowing hair and his chin is her elbow.

Now, what do you see at first glance in the figure below?

Figure 9.4 M.C. Escher's "Circle Limit IV" © 2006 The M.C. Escher Company-Holland. All rights reserved.

Did you see angels or bats? This figure has both. Some immediately see one and some see the other.

These two figures illustrate the notion of separate realities. Two people can look at the exact same image and legitimately see two different things. Usually, the differences are not this simple and clear. Sometimes we will never see what someone else sees in a situation. But that doesn't mean *they* don't see it.

What do you notice in the markings below?[35] Maybe you just see smudges of black on white.

Figure 9.5

Now, suppose someone told you they saw a cowboy on a horse? You could dispute them, dismiss them and move on. Or, if you were a very curious person, or if you really trusted and respected them, you could accept that there was a horse and look for it. If you did, you would probably find it in time. Once you did, it would become very obvious to you. And, if you look back on it anytime in the days or months ahead, the horse will be obvious.

In life, we tend to only see a small portion of what is in front of us: just a few of someone else's personality traits, one way we view a situation, the one decision that's obvious to us, and only a few aspects of a culture.

Recently, a long-time CEO told us he had a great culture with wonderful values. He felt his culture was the strength of the organization. When we asked why he was meeting with us, he said that they were having a hard time implementing a new strategy. When we asked what behaviors were getting in the way, his answer was that there were too many turf issues—people were resisting the change and spending too much time pointing fingers and blaming each other.

That seemed like a paradox to us, so we asked what it was that he felt was so great about the culture. He replied that they had good foundational values like honesty and integrity. When it came to other values that we believe are also important in a culture, like innovation, collaboration and accountability, his company came up short. His definition of culture was integrity; ours was much broader. We were looking at the same thing as the CEO but we saw it as a cultural issue—which he was not able to see until later.

Once you see something in a certain way, you tend to lock in and believe that it is the only way, or "the truth." Research has shown that first impressions are very hard to undo, with many subsequent interactions needed to change first impressions. If you have decided you don't like someone, you will always be more aware of what they do wrong, even though they may do more things right. If you decide "my way" or "my answer" is right, then you can see all its benefits and are less likely to see or hear what may be wrong with it. This is similar to someone locking in on seeing the face on the prior page and not being able to see the woman.

We all have blind spots and selective perception. That is why all those cars of a given type or color magically appear on the highway just when you decide you want to buy one. Or why couples suddenly notice dozens of babies all around them, wherever they go, when they decide they want a family. Selective perception is also the source of most arguments and misunderstandings. When we understand that the principle driving many of our relationship issues is separate realities, we can adjust by recognizing that we overlook things because we see them through our own unique filters. This gives us the humility to be curious, not self-righteous, and to listen more openly to other points of view for something we may have missed.

This concept is the reason wise leaders must respect "the wisdom of the team" and the need for diversity in thinking and points of view in an organization. Someone with a different point of view may be seeing something others are not seeing. One exercise in Senn-Delaney Leadership's seminar really drives this point home. We ask a group to complete a simple task: Count the number of times a specific letter shows up in a paragraph. Eighty percent of the people come up short in their count. Most are absolutely certain they have it right. We've had CFO's and CEO's place large bets that they were right—when they weren't. Few people see all the designated letters because of the way our brain functions in an analytical-task mode. The point is: We all have blind spots, and sometimes when we are absolutely certain we are right about something, we are actually wrong.

David Novak, CEO of Yum! Brands, believes our exercise and the concept of blind spots helped him and his team become more effective. It causes people to be more open to ask questions like, "Are we missing something here?" or "Does someone see it a different way?"

The principles in the Human Operating System have profound implications for personal and professional relationships as well as for team dynamics. If all the team members understand these principles, they can solve problems, discuss strategies, and make decisions faster, easier and more innovatively. They are the foundation for:

- Better listening – "I may be missing something."

- Respectful dialog – "It's my point of view, not a universal truth."

- More innovation – "Let's explore other ways to look at this."

- Less stress – "Worry is just a thought about something that probably won't happen."

As the next chapter shows, insight-generating experiences—such as the exercises described above—allow us to identify our blind spots, selective perceptions, win-lose behaviors and moods. More importantly, these insights help us to become more curious as opposed to righteous and more open to learning rather than defending past beliefs and habits.

QUESTIONS TO CONSIDER

1. How well am I managing my energy? How might I manage it better?

   _____

   _____

   _____

2. Of the thought habits on page 105, which ones do I have? How would my thinking shift to improve my results?

   _____

   _____

   _____

3. Did I see the horse or lady with the baby at first glance? Am I too certain at times that I have the answer?

   _____

   _____

   _____

10

BRINGING THE VALUES TO LIFE: HOW TO UNFREEZE OLD HABITS

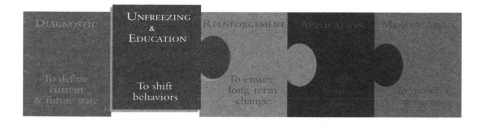

DIAGNOSTIC | UNFREEZING & EDUCATION | REINFORCEMENT | APPLICATION | MEASUREMENT

To define current & future state | To shift behaviors | To ensure long-term change | | To monitor progress

Figure 10.1 © 2006 Senn-Delaney Leadership Consulting Group, LLC.

If thought habits and moods drive our behaviors, how do we change those habits? Culture is nothing more than the collective beliefs and habits of the people in an organization. Shifting these lifelong habits is the fundamental challenge we face in shaping a culture. How do you change the habits of adults? How do you get a seasoned 25-year executive who is over-controlling and territorial to collaborate, delegate and coach? How do you get a culture where people blame others, are inwardly-focused, risk-averse or resistant to change to become more accountable, customer-centric, agile and innovative? Kurt Lewin, Ph.D., an early researcher and writer in the field of organizational development, put it well when he observed:

When we are young we are like a flowing river—and then we freeze.

We believe the secret lies in "unfreezing" old behaviors. This more powerful approach to change is needed because, as many leaders have told us, "The values do hang on the walls, but the desired behaviors aren't fully alive in the halls."

The failure of most culture shaping efforts is that organizations skip the unfreezing step in the change model. They may run diagnostics and analyze survey data. They may define core values and competencies and select a set of leadership behaviors. They may communicate them and hold educational sessions about them. What they fail to do is truly *unfreeze* old behaviors and connect people at a gut level to the Essential Values.

Because people's thinking drives their behaviors, a shift in old, underlying thinking is necessary in order to shift behaviors. Since many of our thought habits are invisible to us, in order to stimulate change, people need a process that enables them to recognize their old habits and gain new insights.

Unfreezing old behaviors is best done through transformational "insight-based" workshops supported by coaching and reinforcement. Traditional training sessions, intellectual lectures by "experts," case studies, 360° feedback assessments and even coaching, as useful as these tools are, won't do it. Unfreezing requires that "ah-ha" moment to create an insight that leads to different thinking and different behavior.

Here is how unfreezing works in the real world, where we learn best by experience: Someone may have been told on numerous occasions that he doesn't listen well. He may have received the same feedback in survey results, or from a friend or coach. He understands the problem intellectually, so why is it that he still doesn't listen? It's a habit, and habits are hard to break. It may be compounded by the fact that he never considered it all that important.

Now imagine that his spouse announces that she is going to divorce him because she can never get his attention. His spouse explains that he not only doesn't listen, but he doesn't appear to care enough to really be present and available; he comes home from work physically, but his head and heart never really leave the office; his mind is elsewhere and he's not tuned into the needs of the people closest to him.

That could be the "ah-ha" moment when he finally hears the message, stops and reflects on its deeper implications and really takes his listening issue seriously. He is then likely to make a gut-level commitment to do something about his behavior.

The concept of rapid behavior change through insightful experiences is not new. You probably know of at least one business executive who has had a significant life event that got their attention—a heart attack, bypass surgery or other health scare. The experience probably changed their perspective on life and changed some of their behaviors.

The overeating workaholic you once knew is now a dedicated walker or runner, and maybe an evangelist about their diet. They may also have a different perspective about how precious life is and become committed to spending quality time with family and friends. Life changed due to a significant emotional experience.

Major physical and emotional experiences often result in a change in how we see the world. The experience can be positive or negative. Personal changes often follow a divorce, the death of a loved one, marriage, a religious experience or the birth of a child. Both positive and negative emotional experiences can cause a person to step back from their old life patterns, reexamine their beliefs and behaviors, and become committed to rebuilding their life with more balance and meaning than before. Even though the dangers of unhealthy eating habits, lack of exercise or poor communication skills may have been known intellectually, a significant emotional event creates a different kind of knowing, which unfreezes old belief systems and leads to an openness to change that didn't exist before.

How does this apply to culture shaping? The "ah-ha moment" approach to change can be used in a positive, renewing and supportive way in a workshop environment as part of a leadership, teambuilding and culture-shaping process.

Our experience shows that insight-based learning is much more effective in shifting culture than great communication programs, informational meetings or inspirational talks. While the information may be excellent, culture shift is not about new ideas or information as much as it is about creating personal change in the people who make up the culture. Individuals learn best when they personally experience something, as opposed to just hearing it, being told about it or reading about it. Culture shaping requires leaders to change their own behaviors, which are a result of their deeply embedded thought habits. In order to shift that thinking, these leaders need to have a significant experience that will "unfreeze" their thought habits and reconnect them to their own healthy core behaviors.

Indeed, in the case of culture shaping, it might be said:

I hear, I understand;

I do, I learn;

I experience, I change!

The win-lose belief discussed in Chapter 9 is just one example of thinking that would benefit from an unfreezing process. There are dozens of other habits which can be unfrozen through experiential workshop exercises designed to induce insights or "ah-ha" moments. New insights cause people to choose to make commitments to healthier, high-performance behaviors. Insight-based exercises can be created for all of the Essential Values—from accountability and change to collaboration and trust. Without this non-traditional approach to gaining commitment to values, culture shaping is hard to accomplish.

While this model makes intuitive sense to people, many executives, especially those in certain cultures, resist the idea of devoting time to what they consider "soft" topics, such as behavior.

Cultures Tend to Resist What They Most Need to Change

Cultures have a way of maintaining the status quo. In science, this is called homeostasis. All living systems have ways of protecting themselves from change. A culture is a living system and its way of avoiding change is to reject people and approaches that seem counter-cultural. For example, cultures that are rational and analytical will only want to accept rational and analytical processes to change the culture. Unfortunately for them, human behaviors and beliefs are not always rational or logical, so that's a recipe for failure.

One accounting firm we worked with wanted to focus almost exclusively on data from our cultural audit and other forms of measurement. An engineering firm seemed compelled to diagram the process and analyze it to death. A financial services firm wanted to focus heavily on financial rewards. In each case, they tended to avoid or initially reject the more personal insight-based training needed to shift behaviors. When we were able to also focus on personal and team behaviors, positive breakthroughs were made.

Models of Behavior Change

There are two primary ways to modify behaviors. The first is behavior modification; i.e., define what you want and reinforce it through activities such as rewards, punishments, coaching and performance appraisals. We believe such reinforcement is important, but not powerful enough on its own to shift culture. (The role of reinforcement in shaping behaviors is further discussed in Chapter 11.)

The second way, which more rapidly shifts behaviors, is the insight-based, experiential change we've been exploring in this chapter. Significant events disrupt our status quo and cause us to question long-held beliefs and habits. In business organizations, the "experience" can come from events such as a bankruptcy filing, a takeover attempt, a precipitous drop in sales or income, fear of job loss, or a competitive attack on the core business. These events also cause a more rapid change in companies. They are externally-driven, however, and often create a reactive, fear-driven response.

Contrary to popular belief, culture shaping can take place without a burning platform. Insights about how a manager can better lead can be systematically created via a positive and renewing seminar experience. Experiential exercises can be designed to give leaders insights into their own behaviors and how they are contributing to the organization's cultural barriers.

Such insights might include "ah-ha's" about "Why I...":

- Tend to be territorial and non-collaborative

- Am so controlling and non-empowering

- Don't give appreciative feedback and coach others

- Tend to be judgmental and see what's wrong with new ideas versus helping build them

- Am so impatient and not a good listener

- Don't hold my people even more accountable

- Am reluctant to take risks

- Worry more than I need to

- Don't share information with others freely enough

- Make excuses when I miss goals

- Don't confront other people and issues more easily

- Struggle with stress and balance in life issues

These insights can lead to shifts in thinking and drive new, healthy, high-performance behaviors such as added openness and trust, respectful candor, better teamwork, increased accountability, less stress, better delegation and increased coaching.

Once individuals truly feel the need for change and experience how much better their business and personal lives can be with new behaviors, they can commit fully and freely to the change process.

To be effective in shifting culture, the unfreezing transformational experience should focus on the values and guiding behaviors that define the desired new culture. By focusing on a set of business values and daily behaviors that spell out success in the new culture, people can begin to live that new culture, practice the new behaviors, discuss the new values and how they apply to work, and gain a comfort and familiarity with the changes being asked of them.

LEADERSHIP AND LIFE EFFECTIVENESS

Research has shown that it is much easier to improve leadership effectiveness when people simultaneously work on life effectiveness. People who don't listen at work probably don't listen at home either. Managers who don't adequately appreciate their employees probably fall short on expressing appreciation for their loved ones as well.

Use of this principle creates a more powerful culture-shaping process and faster behavioral change. That's because when the change process helps us gain insights about principles of life effectiveness as well as leadership effectiveness, we are more likely to want to change ourselves for ourselves, not just for the company. The change then becomes more appealing because it is internally-driven. The change process becomes a "pull," not a "push" system, because it's driven by the wants and needs of people, not the dictates of management.

THE SHORTFALL IN TRAINING

Leadership and teambuilding training is required for rapid culture shaping; unfortunately, all too many organizations see training as the first thing to cut when budgets get tight. In high-performing organizations like GE, training and workout sessions are seen as vital to business success, not just "nice to do, when we get some extra time or money!"

A lack of more support for training is understandable because many of the more traditional training processes are marginally effective. In contrast, insight-based training that unfreezes old behaviors around the Essential Values is imperative for behavior change and thus cultural change.

A common mistake in training is starting with the wrong groups at the wrong level. In many companies, the top teams often view training as something for the people "under them." They may not have been deeply impacted by training in many years, if ever, so the value of any training, much less an insight-based training, is an intellectual concept. This is a challenge to culture shaping because of the *shadow of the leader* phenomenon. Until the top leaders have a deeply meaningful experience themselves, their support for training will remain merely intellectual and the shadow they cast won't change. This makes the training at lower levels less effective.

In short, culture-shaping processes need to start at the top. If you have ever launched an important training initiative at levels below the senior teams, you have probably heard comments from participants like, "My boss could use this" or "This sounds great, but it's not the way they lead us."

Leadership training in many organizations focuses primarily on "high performers." While that is useful to develop individuals, it doesn't shape the culture. The same is true for training focused on skill-building, or university-expert programs with case studies. All this training, while useful, is more *informational* than *transformational* and thus has little impact on the overall culture.

The reality is that training of any kind is too often seen as "discretionary" and subject to budget swings. At the same time, companies will spend millions on ERP, CRM systems or other change initiatives that will end up over budget, behind schedule, and short of expectations because companies have not invested in eliminating the "jaws of culture."

The missing ingredient in almost all culture-shaping initiatives is the unfreezing step. It's like trying to bake the perfect loaf of bread but leaving out the yeast—it simply won't rise. A lot of good work can be done in culture shaping, but if the process is not transformational, meaningful change is unlikely to follow.

QUESTIONS TO CONSIDER

1. What habits from pages 119 would you like to "unfreeze" in yourself?

_____

_____

_____

_____

_____

2. What habits would you like to unfreeze in a team you are on or in your organization?

_____

_____

_____

_____

_____

11

REINFORCEMENT: A KEY TO SUSTAINING BEHAVIOR CHANGE

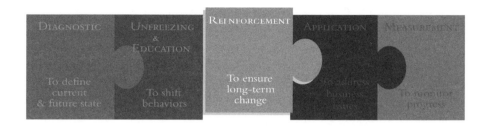

Figure 11.1 © 2006 Senn-Delaney Leadership Consulting Group, LLC.

Have you ever made a resolution to change that you didn't keep? Have you been inspired by a speech, book or seminar, but then the inspiration faded? We all have experienced new insights and then made commitments that didn't take hold.

This gap between what you commit to and what you actually do usually results from the lack of ongoing reinforcement and clear consequences. It is not enough to unfreeze old behaviors and gain commitments to new ones. Any change in habit requires ongoing reminders and reinforcement.

Making culture change a way of life requires that you approach change as a long-term process, not just "this year's initiative." You may take two steps forward and one step back, but if you have a deep commitment to change, constant reminders and reinforcement can help get you there.

Most behavior change efforts fail because of the disconnected initiatives syndrome. To shape a culture, all reinforcement systems need to be aligned. One common example is an organization with a teamwork value when compensation plans pay only for individual performance.

The Role Reinforcement Has in Change

In the previous chapters we discussed one school of thought about change. That theory holds that significant life events create insights into new ways of seeing the world, and this enlightenment creates change. That is what we called "unfreezing."

A second theory of change, promoted by "behavioral reinforcement" advocates, contends that if you define what you want and reinforce it long enough and well enough, behavior will change. This age-old school includes researchers like Pavlov, whose dogs learned to salivate when they heard a bell since food usually followed this signal and Skinner, who taught mice to run through a maze for a reward.

Most attempts at shifting behaviors in corporations follow this behavioral-reinforcement model. It places heavy emphasis on communications, HR systems and rewards. We believe change is most successful if you combine both approaches in the right sequence, because new insights are often prerequisites for change; however, they don't ensure that change can be sustained.

Organizational Reinforcement

If you want specific values and behaviors to be a way of life in an organization, all systems that influence people need to support those same values. Well-designed training can provide gut-level buy-in, but continuous reinforcement needs to occur, in many forms, to make it an ongoing way of life.

The most effective organizational reinforcement systems reside in Human Resources (HR). Too often, training programs alone are expected to change behavior. Unless the HR systems, policies and procedures are aligned with the new cultural values, old behaviors tend to persist.

HR Cultural Reinforcement systems include:

- A selection process that screens candidates for the desired values and behaviors

- A new-employee orientation process that stresses the culture

- A performance management process with values and behaviors as a part of reviews

- A compensation system that provides incentives for living the values

- A succession planning process with promotions tied to living the values as well as making the numbers

There are so many touch points for culture that we urge clients to form a "Culture Action Team" with representatives from HR, communications and other groups. The team's job is to look at all of the ways the values can be reinforced through systems and communications.

The front of the chain is on-boarding. Hiring profiles can be developed to assist managers in selecting people who are a match for the values. At Senn-Delaney Leadership, we put a high premium on hiring people who are accountable, collaborative and have a strong desire to make a positive difference at this point in their lives. It is important for us to select people with diverse backgrounds and different styles but with a core belief set that includes our values.

Some clients have pre-hiring materials that describe the organization's culture and behavioral expectations of employees. Others do a great job at cultural orientation for new hires. The same examination should be made of all systems.

COMPENSATION AND GOAL-SETTING

Perhaps the most challenging system to tackle is compensation. To align team behaviors, the compensation systems, as well as, the reward and recognition systems must shift from the traditional focus on individual performance to an increased focus on team and company performance. This requires a review of the entire compensation program, including salary, bonus and incentive plans, as well as job descriptions, to ensure that collaborative behaviors are properly rewarded.

The appraisal system also provides important reinforcement, and carries more weight when you tie compensation to living the values. For example, an energy-services client tied one-third of the potential performance bonus to a combination of living the values and implementing the new culture. Bell Atlantic CEO Ray Smith tied 30% of leaders' bonuses to how well they were living and leading the *Bell Atlantic Way* behaviors.

Another key system change that greatly impacts culture and employee behaviors is goal setting, particularly in the budgeting process. A CFO for a major East Coast bank attended a Senn-Delaney Leadership seminar along with the other senior officers during their annual budget process. Before the shared offsite experience, he and others complained how difficult it was to convince people to cooperate and share resources to arrive at the rolled-up budget figures. "Everybody was out to protect their own department, and no one was willing to give up resources, people or dollars to support another area of the bank. I've been through dozens of these wars. We finally arrived at a good budget, but the conflict and gamesmanship gets old!"[36]

Following the senior management's culture-change seminar, the CFO and his senior team finished the budget easily. They hadn't talked about the budget during the offsite seminar, but they did agree to a new set of team behaviors to help them focus on what was good for the overall corporation—not just one department. Because they learned and practiced these new behaviors—specifically support and trust—during the seminar, they were able to repeat them during the budgeting process, and the behaviors quickly became the new norm at the top of the organization.

One of the strongest cultural signals is "who gets promoted and why?" In many ways, the culture is defined and the rules for success are contained in the promotion policies and examples. If promotions occur because of loyalty and tenure, this sends confusing signals about what behaviors are being rewarded. If leaders preach that "teamwork is an important value," but then promote someone who is known to be a poor team player, their words carry little meaning.

A large insurance client tied their new cultural values and guiding behaviors to the succession-planning process. In fact, the final decision to move the president into the CEO's role was, in part, dependent upon the Board and the retiring CEO's confidence that the new leader could effectively model and perpetuate the newly emerging culture, which was seen as a competitive advantage. This was also true of a large aerospace/defense client who revamped their entire leadership assessment and succession-planning system to include their new values and guiding behaviors.

Whatever measures or reinforcement tools you use, the key to your success is the spirit and commitment with which you apply these tools.

Leaders need to commit to personal growth, facilitate growth in others, support the changes needed in reinforcement systems, and use them to drive culture shaping.

Disconnected Initiatives Syndrome

All organizations have reinforcement systems; however, in most companies these systems are not tied together, nor are they mutually reinforcing. We call this the *disconnected initiatives syndrome*. It looks like this: Leadership competencies measure one set of skills or behaviors, but the corporate values don't fully match that set, and the 360° feedback instrument measures something else altogether. The performance review process stresses teamwork, but the compensation system rewards individual contributions. People are recruited based on one set of behaviors and experiences, and then promoted on another. It may all "sort of" match, but not well enough to shape a culture. In the absence of aligned reinforcement systems, the organization will often sustain an undesirable culture with internal competition, entitlement and lack of innovation.

To make matters worse, business unit leaders may follow one set of behaviors to successfully implement their strategies, while leadership development training focuses on something else. The most common disconnect occurs in a shared services model that depends on people making sacrifices for the greater organizational good, while the majority of bonuses are paid for individual unit performance.

A successful culture-shaping initiative requires reinforcement that is consistent and fully aligned with the needed behaviors. That is why an aligned and integrated HR plan is so vital to any major change process.

Coaching and Feedback as Reinforcement

The most direct and powerful reinforcement a leader can receive is coaching and feedback. The cheapest, easiest and yet most neglected tool for behavioral change is positive reinforcement. When people are appreciated for doing something approximately right, they will repeat the behavior.

Nurturing new behaviors in a culture requires catching people doing things approximately right. We sometimes point out to leaders that babies would never learn to talk or walk if they were treated as many leaders treat their employees. Toddlers make a lot of mistakes at the start. Fortunately, doting parents and grandparents are the ones who coach babies as they learn to walk and talk. Anything close to a step or a word receives appreciative feedback, and progress always follows.

If you are helping someone shift a behavior, one of the best things you can do is appreciate even small steps in the right direction. This is in keeping with all the research ever done on behavioral reinforcement. Positive reinforcement creates better, faster results than negative reinforcement.

Some clients focus on using appreciative feedback to create a recognition culture. In addition to shaping behaviors, it is also the express button on the Mood Elevator. A recognition culture makes a great place to work, and that means a better experience for customers.

A feedback-rich environment is important for behavior change and cultural change. Not only do people need appreciative feedback, but they also need *constructive* feedback when they are not walking the talk. If leaders who influence the organization behave in ways that are counter to the desired culture they need to be (respectfully) called on it; otherwise they will damage the change effort. In extreme cases, leaders who don't walk the talk will need to leave the organization if their behavior doesn't change. The reason is clear: The employees will observe the leader's behavior as acceptable, even if it conflicts with the stated values and guiding behaviors.

WHY WE DON'T DO MORE COACHING

Coaching and feedback should take place on a day-to-day, cash-and-carry basis between bosses and direct reports, direct reports and bosses, and between peers. We all know it is important, so why don't we do more of it?

There are many thought habits or beliefs that contribute to the shortage of feedback:

- *"I don't have time."*

- *"They may think my praise is insincere."*

- *"They don't need it."*

- *"That's their job."*

- *"I don't want to hurt their feelings."*

To reshape a culture, you need to unfreeze these beliefs about coaching and replace them with new thinking:

- *"My job is to be a coach."*

- *"I'll let them down if I don't coach them."*

- *"I'll save time in the long run by developing them now."*

Appreciation is not soft stuff. It not only lifts people's spirits, it raises their performance level.

EXECUTIVE COACHING

Having an executive coach has become very popular. It makes sense to invest in the development of your most senior leaders and high performers. Leaders have blind spots like everyone else.

Coaching top leaders is important because of another phenomenon: The higher a leader gets in the company, the fewer people s/he feels free to confide in. There are also fewer people who will take the perceived risk of giving the leader constructive feedback. This can lead to the "emperor without clothes" syndrome. An outside coach can be candid and help minimize blind spots.

There is a flaw, however, in most traditional executive coaching models. It is based too much on "telling," which is informational, not transformational. Leaders have deeply embedded habits. They are almost always well-intentioned and really just doing what makes sense to them based on their own thinking. Just telling a leader how to behave differently is not enough to successfully change their behavior. However, if you can assist a leader in changing their *thinking*, which drives their behavior, the behavior itself will change.

One striking example comes to mind. It happened during an executive coaching session with a competent and hard-driving CEO, as part of a larger culture-change process. Earlier in his career he had been trained under a CEO who was very harsh. As a result, he developed a belief that the tougher he got, the more results he would get. While he had received feedback that his behavior was at times inappropriate and often counter-productive, he didn't change his pattern.

After we developed a high level of trust and rapport with the CEO, he began to understand that we wanted the same thing he did—results. At that point, we began to explore his belief about his need for an extremely demanding style. We confirmed that he had a clear-cut mental model: "The more demanding I am, the more results I will get." We asked him if that behavior consistently got him what he wanted. It didn't and he knew it.

What he came to realize was that, up to a point, his high expectations inspired exceptional results. Beyond that point, especially when he became angry and abusive, the results fell off. Once he had that "ah-ha," he began to understand that his anger and intimidation was turning his team against him and creating nonproductive, passive-aggressive behaviors in them and the organization. Through a dialog process, his thinking changed to a new belief: "I get the best results by maintaining and demanding high standards, but when I 'go over the edge' I lose my effectiveness and impede results."

The mental picture he now holds is shown in the figure below (Figure 11.2).

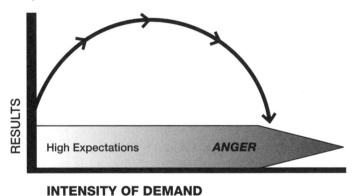

INTENSITY OF DEMAND

Figure 11.2 © 2006 Senn-Delaney Leadership Consulting Group, LLC.

With coaching, he learned to read the signals that told him where he was on the curve: his feeling or mood. All he had to do was look to his feeling or mood as his guide. The tool he used to do that was the Mood Elevator. When he felt extreme intensity or anger, this was his clue that his thinking was not as reliable. He knew that his words or actions might not be appropriate nor effective and it was a time to take a deep breath and cool off, if possible, before acting.

It was just the opposite with another CEO who hesitated too long to call the shots. There were too many unresolved issues that he needed to address and his team was frustrated that he wouldn't make the necessary decisions. The coaching process revealed that at one point in his career he had worked for a leader who was extremely controlling and had stifled his creativity and discouraged initiative. He vowed he would never be that way and adopted an overly consensus-driven style of leadership. We also found that he didn't like the discomfort he felt when he had to displease others with his decisions.

His style had worked well when he had a team that easily came to consensus. However, his current team was not that way. They had some legitimate differences in point of view, and as a result decisions dragged on and on. With some coaching from us and reinforcement from a number of his team members, he had a shift in thinking. He realized he was not like his earlier boss, as he naturally gave people a lot of latitude. He also realized that he was letting his team and organization down by not dealing with the "elephants in the room" that only he could deal with. He needed to be OK with some discomfort for the greater good of the organization. As a result, he and the team performed much better.

Coaching is an important part of reinforcement. Coaching to the level of thinking and state of mind or mood of the person being coached, as in these examples, has a much more powerful impact.

USE OF SYMBOLIC REMINDERS

When people are anchored in a meaningful experience, even a small reminder can be powerful. Just think of a meaningful event in your life. You probably associate it with a sound, song, word, smell or picture that represents that experience. When you encounter that symbolic sensory reminder, you are suddenly drawn back to that event and what it represents to you.

Symbolic reminders that follow an experiential learning process do the same thing. If a symbol or visual image reminds you of the importance of being a team player, for example, keeping that symbol where you can see it will help you achieve that new behavior. Many clients have used this concept well. The Tennessee Valley Authority (TVA) created clever screensavers with reminders of the behaviors from their Star 7 cultural transformation initiative.

Language can also play a similar reminder role. In fact, culture is, in part, rooted in language. A simple phrase like "let's try to make this win-win vs. win-lose" can change the nature of an interaction or a meeting if all parties are grounded in the same experience and concept.

Our clients find that many other phrases from their culture-shaping seminar become part of the company vocabulary. Some examples include:

- Where we are on the Mood Elevator?

- Assume best intentions.

- Listen for understanding.

- What I appreciate about you is...

- Let's not be observer-critics.

- What more can we do to get the result?

As a part of their process to move from being semi-autonomous regional telephone companies to one unified global competitor, Bell Atlantic used a symbolic figure that looked like a puzzle to remind everyone they were a part of a bigger game. That game, which taught the lesson of playing for the bigger win, was played in the cultural workshops managers had attended. The CEO attributed part of the success of the cultural transformation to the use of this symbol and the shared seminar experience that connected everyone to it.

Personal Reminders and Communications

An ongoing flow of communications and brief reminder messages can play an important role in reinforcing behavior change in employees. Stories about successes, along with messages from their leader, help keep the concepts alive.

Another powerful new tool is the electronic reminder. We have developed one we call eCoach®. Email is a great vehicle to remind people of new behaviors. In our experience, soft-side leadership skills do not lend themselves well to eLearning as a *replacement* for face-to-face interventions. Leadership is a contact sport. On the other hand, online messages are a great way to provide reminders of *what has been learned*, especially if the reminders are brief, interesting, hard-hitting and are used to reconnect people to a previous meaningful experience.

Senior leaders can also send powerful reinforcement messages by publicly recognizing others in their organizations for achieving strong results while living the values. These stories become powerful reminders to all employees of how they, too, can utilize the values while getting excellent results.

Action Steps

Here are some ways to use reinforcement if you want to create changes in yourself, your team, your company or your family:

1. Practice using appreciative feedback. Do a better job of catching people at work and at home doing things approximately right and recognizing them.

2. Make a commitment to coach a direct report, peer and your boss in relation to living the values. Let them know what you appreciate and how they could be even more effective.

3. Create a reminder for yourself of an idea from this book. Use the Mood Elevator or another symbol or set of words to remind you of concepts you want to embrace.

4. Create an "I will" statement about a behavior you want to work on. Keep it where you will notice it frequently as a reminder.

5. Check to see if your company is following the advice in this chapter on organizational reinforcement. Do you have disconnected initiatives? Are your company's values a part of the screening process you or others use when hiring new employees?

12

THE PAYOFF—APPLYING THE PRINCIPLES

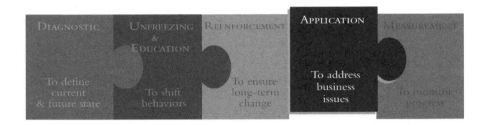

DIAGNOSTIC	UNFREEZING & EDUCATION	REINFORCEMENT	APPLICATION	MEASUREMENT
To define current & future state	To shift behaviors	To ensure long-term change	To address business issues	To monitor progress

Figure 12.1 © 2006 Senn-Delaney Leadership Consulting Group, LLC.

"USE IT OR LOSE IT"

An overwhelming amount of evidence exists that people retain new learning far better if they put it into practice. That is why application—using the values and behaviors to create results—is the fourth pillar of culture shaping. You can define your guiding behaviors and reinforce them, but to get results you have to apply them in the real world. The added benefit is that when people use elements of the new culture to create real and tangible results, they more quickly adopt the new behaviors.

TVA demonstrated this very well. They made great progress in shifting behaviors in the organization through their innovative culture-shaping process, Star 7. Despite the measurable behavior shifts, there were still a number of people who thought that work on a "soft topic" like culture didn't have enough bottom-line connection. In response, they developed the Translating Values to Action process we describe in Chapter 5. By developing what they called "line of sight" from each group to the overall critical success factors, they identified measurable goals that would contribute directly to a limited number of critical overall corporate initiatives.

They then identified the shifts in behavior needed to support that tangible initiative. For example:

- How could TVA better apply the accountability value to stretch goals vs. blaming other functions?

- With what groups did they need to improve their collaboration to better implement a process?

- In what areas did they need to innovate or be more open to change to create more breakthroughs?

By connecting the values to specific deliverable goals, they accomplished several things. They improved results, they demonstrated how culture makes a difference and they made believers out of even the most skeptical leaders.

Getting results using the corporate values validates the importance of developing a high-performance culture. Remember, culture really does have a return on investment. Taking the time to create a healthy culture pays off in tangible, measurable business results.

That is why Application is the fourth element in the change model. All three approaches to behavior change are illustrated in the figure below (Figure 12.2). It shows symbolically how unfreezing to gain insights, plus reinforcement and application, is the model for successful change.

Combining Unfreezing, Reinforcement and Application

Behavior Change Requires All Three

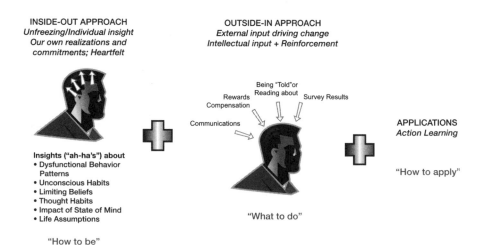

Figure 12.2 © 2006 Senn-Delaney Leadership Consulting Group, LLC.

Applications, as used in the DURAM™ culture-change model we've been describing, simply means using the behaviors that define the desired culture to get results. For example, people may get great insights about a value like collaboration in a culture-shaping seminar. They may have those insights reinforced through coaching and communications. When they finally collaborate in new ways and get a better result, the value of collaboration becomes real to them and they adopt the new behavior.

The *application* element of the DURAM™ change model is based on the belief that we either "use it or lose it." Whatever we put into practice, or apply, becomes a part of us. When teams and individuals use new, healthy, high-performance behaviors to get better results, they validate the behaviors and create new behavioral patterns.

Applications take place at three levels:

- *The individual level,* where people live the values to get more results

- *The team level,* where winning teams use the values as "rules of the road" for working together to achieve more

- *The organizational level,* where high-performance teams collaborate across the organization to better execute corporate strategies and implement critical systems and initiatives

INDIVIDUAL APPLICATION

Individual applications focus on how each person can live the values on a daily basis and thus influence their team and the culture. Since the shadow of each leader has such a powerful influence on teams and organizations, the first area of application is at the individual level.

APPLYING THE MOOD ELEVATOR

Of all the Essential Values, the one that provides the greatest advantage is *a healthy state of mind.* When your state of mind or mood is higher, you operate at your best and more naturally exhibit all the essential values. You can apply this concept to advantage at work and at home. You can start by monitoring your own energy when encountering others and when you are in team meetings or having discussions with people.

Check your Mood Elevator when you walk in the door at work in the morning or at home in the evening. Are you generating positive energy when engaging those around you?

Now that you know the impact of your moods on the quality of your thinking, learn to read your moods through your feelings. Monitor the Mood Elevator and determine where you are on that elevator when working with your team. When your mood state is low, know that your thinking is unreliable and look for assistance from your teammates. Solicit their input and delegate when possible.

Practicing Being in the Now

The notion of living life more in the present moment is one way to be at your best more often. Being more present with a quieter mind can reduce your stress, increase your creativity and productivity and improve your relationships at work and home. Practicing Be Here Now requires that you avoid three types of distractions (see Figure 12.3).

First, when your thinking starts drifting into the past with thoughts like regret or spinning in the future with worry, take a deep breath and refocus on the person or task at hand. As you get better at this, your natural state of Be Here Now will return.

Second, when your thinking centers on "you," your ego or self-image (i.e., how will this affect me, what is being done to me, how will I look to others), know that this, too, is a sign of drifting from Be Here Now. By recognizing that you are off-track, you allow your mind to re-center itself in the moment. When it is "all about you," you've lost your connection to others. When you are focused on a higher goal or purpose, you are more centered and present.

Third, limit your multi-tasking. If you think that makes you more efficient, that is an illusion. Recent research has shown that multi-tasking actually makes us less effective; momentarily lowering your IQ.[36]

Figure 12.3 © 2006 Senn-Delaney Leadership Consulting Group, LLC.

In contrast, during those moments when you are able to really focus, be present and in the flow, you get breakthrough ideas and a lot more done. When you are hectic and scattered, you may feel busy and important but you probably aren't very productive; at the end of the day, you feel tired and ask yourself, "What did I really get done today?" Distractions take the form of BlackBerries during meetings, working on emails during conference calls and watching TV while talking to loved ones.

Use the Mood Elevator as a guide to how well you are feeling in the present. The lower levels of the Mood Elevator are created by busier thinking, including worry, anger and judgment. The higher levels of the Mood Elevator are characterized by a quieter mind that exists where you are flexible, hopeful, creative and grateful. It's a self-reinforcing behavior: When you are in the higher levels, you are generally being here now; and when you are being here now, you are better able to stay in the higher levels.

Becoming a Better Change Agent

Change is another one of the Essential Values. Do you want to be a better change agent and develop and implement more new ideas in your group? If so, take a look at where you go on the Mood Elevator when you are presented with new ideas. Do you, or those you influence, tend to go to the judgment level too quickly? Do you primarily see what's wrong, or do you explore the possibilities? If you can make it a habit of going to the curious level first, you will find many more useful applications for new ideas.

One reason we don't see more new applications is that we all have blind spots. As you encounter other people and events in your environment, remember that your personal thought filters are at work. Since your filters create your separate reality of events, you need to be aware that you have only one view of each situation. In order to gain a more complete picture, you must solicit input from others and your team. Remind yourself that you may miss seeing things others may see that could lead to new ideas and applications.

One leader who communicates with his team mostly by email sends important messages to a couple of trusted teammates to review before he sends them out to their intended audience. He asks his teammates to read the messages for anything he is not seeing or issues he should take into account. This process creates better communication and builds trust among teammates. It is another application of the principle of "the wisdom of the team."

Just like the old adage says, "change needs to start with me." The same is true in applying the behaviors in a redefined culture. Each person is accountable to use the concepts on a day-to-day basis at work and at home.

QUESTIONS TO CONSIDER

1. What concepts in this book would most benefit you and those you influence if successfully applied?

2. Would you like to be a better change agent? If so, how do you respond to new ideas presented to you—with curiosity or judgment?

3. How well are you doing at being present at work? How about at home? Are you multi-tasking too much?

13

APPLICATIONS FOR TEAMS: WINNING TEAMS CREATE WINNING CULTURES

The building block of a company's culture is the team. In today's complex world, one person can rarely make it happen; teams are needed to get the job done. High-performance teams working collaboratively across the organization form a winning culture.

A team can be a traditional intact team as seen on an organization chart, or it can also be a project team, a special-purpose team or a virtual team. They are simply a group of people with a common goal to achieve.

If you are a leader of a team, take the test in Chapter 4 on the *Eight Characteristics of a High-Performance Team*. It will help you identify any areas of improvement you need to work on. Have a discussion with your team and see if you can make a team agreement around those areas that need more attention.

One question that is difficult to answer with either a yes or a no is, "Do we walk the talk by living the values?" As a group you may be doing well on some, and not so well on others, so it is worthwhile to do a team self-assessment on each of the five Essential Values we have been discussing:

1. The Performance Value

The essence of the performance value is accountability. Individuals may be accountable, but do all team members feel accountable for each other's success? Are they as committed to initiatives led by other team members as they are to the initiatives they lead? Do they feel accountable to help a teammate succeed? Those things represent application of accountability at the team level. Without them, the team can't execute as well.

2. The Collaborative Value

Most good teams collaborate fairly well within the team. Great teams collaborate well across the organization. Line organizations work well with the staff functions and play win-win with other line organizations. Support functions are aligned within, and know that the most successful organizations are "line-led and staff-supported." How well does your team collaborate with other teams?

3. The Change Value

Teams develop reputations as idea-generators or idea-killers. Which one is your team? Team meetings are where new ideas are either killed or nurtured. When your team is presented with a new idea, especially from a lower-level group, are you "observer-critics" or "participant-coaches"? Useful questions to ask your team include:

- Do we tend to point out all the things that are wrong, or do we look for the seeds of new ideas that can move the organization forward?

- Do team members build on the ideas of others or are our meetings just presentations where each person sticks to their own sandbox?

- Do we have any time to be creative or are we just rushed to cover all the topics on the agenda?

4. The Ethics and Integrity Value

Despite all the highly publicized integrity issues at Enron and elsewhere, the vast majority of teams we know score high on fundamental ethics and integrity.

However, there are two related areas where many teams aren't as effective. The first is how well they are perceived by those a few levels down to live the organization's values. When a person or team is not living the values, they are, in a sense, "out of integrity." Even the smallest deviations are noted and in fact magnified by the people looking up. That is why the team should look very closely at how they are walking the talk and how that is seen from below.

The second related shortfall in integrity is lack of openness and candor. There are many teams that have people who are polite but not honest and direct with one another. They may disagree with an idea in a meeting but just smile and say nothing. Later they will probably tell someone how they feel, but not the person who brought up the idea. Great teams are respectful as well as open and direct. They have written or unwritten ground rules that call for directness in communications. This eliminates the normal corporate hidden agenda and builds high levels of trust. It also enables a team to capture more of the wisdom of the team and make better decisions.

5. The Organizational (Team) Health Value

Teams, like people, operate at different levels of the Mood Elevator. All teams have their rough moments but what is the norm for yours?

- What is the energy level of your team? High or low?

- Is the team hopeful and optimistic or pessimistic?

- What is the shadow of the team's mood?

The effectiveness of your meetings and the quality of your decisions is directly proportionate to the mood of the team in the meeting. If you are judgmental, worried, impatient or low-energy, the meeting won't go as well. If any of the team members are self-righteous, assuming motives or not really present, it will impact the quality of your meetings and your decisions. It will impact your ability to execute as a unified team. How is your team's health?

Making Team Meetings Effective (Putting the Values to Use)

The most obvious place to put the Essential Values to use is in team meetings. Almost all our clients agree that they have too many meetings that take too much of their time and create too little value. Together with emails, meetings are the biggest reason we work so long, feel so hectic and lack balance in our lives. The teams that master the art and science of healthy, high-performance meetings have a major competitive advantage.

Because of the importance of meetings and the need for them to be more effective, Senn-Delaney Leadership has developed some high-performance team models that really make a difference. One model is designed to address the dynamics, or human factors, in a meeting. The team's habitual behavior in meetings represents the *culture of the team*; and as we have established, the culture determines the team's success or failure.

Like culture, team dynamics are often invisible to us. We are much more aware of the content of a meeting but are hampered by the underlying human dynamics. These include:

- Are people present or are they on their BlackBerries?

- Are people really listening to each other?

- Do some people dominate the discussion and others not speak up?

- Does the discussion wander or does it stay on point?

- Are issues brought to closure or left unresolved?

The Healthy Meeting Dynamics model is based on the team members agreeing to do their best to:

Operate from feelings of goodwill in the higher levels of the Mood Elevator

One way to promote this model is to use the first five or ten minutes of a meeting to deliberately create some positive energy and ensure people are really mentally present. This could include sharing a success story, celebrating a win, taking some time for appreciative feedback or discussing a cultural value.

The leader, a designated member or the entire team accepts accountability to monitor the tone of the meeting. Where are we on the Mood Elevator? If we are heading downward, or the conversation is wandering and the energy dropping, someone needs to call it out. If you hit the basement and seem stuck, call a brief break so people can clear their heads. Most groups keep grinding and grinding while they get less and less productive. It is amazing how much more gets done after a break, when the energy has come back up.

Listen for understanding and assume best intentions in team-mates

When we ask people participating in our workshops to list the things they know they need to work on, the two most common items are patience and listening. The lack of better listening skills has a negative impact on most meetings.

As you go from one meeting to the next, stop for a few seconds, take a deep breath and simply remind yourself to "Be present." Respectful listening with an openness to be influenced is a key component of winning teams.

One of the filters that distorts our ability to listen is the assumption of the motives of our teammates. A foundational principle of all *winning* teams is an assumption that fellow teammates are well-intentioned; that they, too, want the company to win. They may legitimately see things differently, but they rarely have negative intentions. Recognize that everyone is doing the best they can, and are operating from their own filters based on how they see the world. Resist assigning motives to team members or others and seek to understand the thinking behind the actions.

Speak up respectfully from your "point of view," not your "truth"

Some people simply don't speak up much in meetings. That's OK if they feel they can't add materially to the topic because it has already been covered. If everyone talked about everything, meetings would take even longer. We have some clients whose team members merely say "ditto" when they agree with something that has been said.

A problem arises if people don't speak up when they have a better idea or see something important being missed, or—more importantly—when they have a strong point of view they will voice later in the hall.

In contrast, there may be other people who speak up as if they have the truth or "the" answer; and in doing so they communicate in a way that doesn't leave much room for others' viewpoints. It's important for everyone to remember that we all have filters and blind spots. Ideas flow much better in meetings when people are respectful and show openness to others by using language like "the way it appears to me" or "from my point of view."

Seek agreement in principle before debating the details

We have observed many meetings where people were in total agreement about a direction, but it was impossible to tell that from the conversation. No one ever said, "so we all agree that we will do X; now we just have to finalize the details." All that could be heard was the disagreement about some of the details.

While it may not seem important, stopping to get what we call *agreement in principle* makes a big difference in meetings. It often takes just a moment, but it raises the tone, lets everyone know they are on the same page and makes the discussion about what can be important differences in execution much healthier and more productive.

Make decisions for the greater good

When teams come together, everyone needs to take off one hat and put on another. The hat they need to leave at the door is the self-serving one: "How can I best defend my group?"; "How will this affect me?"; "How can I gain an advantage?"

The hat people need to wear represents an agreement to make decisions for the greater good: "Will we do better overall if I give in on this one?" or "How does what I am proposing impact others?" The strength of a team is only realized if the team commits to this principle.

Healthy Meeting Dynamics Model

- The group strives for a feeling of goodwill – Mood Elevator
- People "listen to understand"
  - ◊ From curiosity vs. judgment
  - ◊ Assuming positive intention
- People speak up if they have a meaningful difference
  - ◊ Speak from point of view
  - ◊ Don't debate "mild preferences"
- People seek "agreement in principle" vs. debating details
- People come from best interest of overall organization vs. self-interest

---

Figure 13.1 © 2006 Senn-Delaney Leadership Consulting Group, LLC.

THE ALIGNMENT DECISION MODEL

A second team application related to meetings is decision-making. With the pace of business more decisions have to be made faster. Delaying decisions too long can bog a company down. However, making them quickly without buy-in and unqualified support from team members can damage execution. The Healthy Meeting Dynamics model on the previous page (Figure 13.1) does a lot to prevent this. In addition, a team needs an explicit model for making decisions that everyone agrees to.

We believe that the Alignment Model is the most effective. It is not a consensus model where everyone must agree to a decision. It is not a democratic model where the most votes wins, nor is it a hierarchical model where everyone just does what the leader says without debate or discussion. So what is it?

The Alignment Model (Figure 13.2 on next page) combines some elements of all those models in a way that:

- Best assures buy-in and ownership

- Avoids blind spots

- Captures the wisdom of the team

The basic concept is that team members, especially those most affected by a decision, should have an opportunity to voice their point of view. All team members should listen with an openness to be influenced, i.e., willing to modify parts of the decision. That dialog often moves the idea to a higher level. Even if two different people start out making a case for A vs. B, the end result, done right, is not a compromise, but an even better answer, or C.

The need for a decision model becomes apparent when consensus is not reached around A, B or C. Well-intentioned people do disagree. If a team uses a consensus model they can become paralyzed. A voting model is not a good choice because it takes accountability for leadership away from the leader and the leader needs to have the final say.

Once team members have had their say, and the pros and cons have been discussed, the decision is up to the leader. At that point the decision leader, usually the team leader, has two choices. They can *defer* the decision or they can *make* the decision. There are legitimate reasons for deferring. One is that the discussion has raised some new questions that need to be answered, or it has revealed the need for new data.

The choice about how quickly the leader "calls the shot" is a stylistic one. Some make decisions quickly and on the spot. In contrast, we have known a number of very successful leaders who make it a habit to "sleep on it" before making a decision. It may take more than one night, but it usually doesn't take long. These leaders have learned that if they take in all the input and then let go of it, an answer often clicks that they feel good about. They simply want to give some time for their wisdom to surface.

The Alignment Model

- Points of view are voiced
- People listen for understanding
- Action follows; either:
  - ◊ Consensus is gained through respectful discussion
  - ◊ Action is deferred
  - ◊ Leader makes decisions
- Once made, all support the *decision* 100%

Figure 13.2 © 2006 Senn-Delaney Leadership Consulting Group, LLC.

Team Together

The final step in the Alignment Model is where many teams fall apart. Once a decision is made, all team members need to own it as though it were their own. For example, if asked about the decision, the answer is "we decided." The reason this is so important is that when all team members' full energy and commitment is put behind a decision, chances are it will succeed. It doesn't matter if "my idea" might have been just a little bit better. We'll never know. What is known is that alignment gets results because energy is focused.

The principles of effective team dynamics outlined in this chapter are applied to specific business issues such as:

- Meeting and exceeding group commitments to the organization

- Determining priorities

- Meeting sales goals and/or budgets

- Implementing important initiatives

- Deciding business strategy

Many special-purpose, virtual and cross-organizational teams can use these concepts to perform better. Examples of special-purpose teams include:

- Merger and acquisition integration teams

- Business process improvement teams

- Systems design and implementation teams

- Customer service teams

- Special project teams

The title of this book, *Winning Teams–Winning Cultures* is a very deliberate one. Healthy, high-performance teams working collaboratively across the organization create a winning culture. It starts with each individual, but the building block is the team.

The culture created by teams collaborating across the organization can be used to drive organizational priorities.

QUESTIONS TO CONSIDER

1. How does my team do on the Eight Characteristics of a High-Performance Team?

   _____

   _____

   _____

2. Which of the Essential Values do we live best and which could use some work?

   _____

   _____

   _____

3. How effective are our meetings? What tips from the Healthy Meeting Dynamics Model could we use?

   _____

   _____

   _____

4. What is our decision model? How clear are we on it?

   _____

   _____

   _____

14

ORGANIZATIONAL APPLICATIONS — CULTURE DRIVES YOUR STRATEGIES

"Culture eats strategy for breakfast."

Sign in the "war room" of Ford Motor Company[37]

STRATEGY

The ideal culture is one that supports an organization's overall mission, strategies and organization-wide initiatives. Whenever an organization wants to shift direction, implement a new strategy, change their structure or execute a new system, culture comes into play. The airline industry, Southwest Airlines in particular, provides a great example of that.

Southwest's culture is one that clearly supports its strategy. This has led to Southwest consistently being a winning organization. That is understandable, because firms with long-term success usually have cultures aligned to support their strategy and structure.

Southwest is a low-cost airline that executes rapid turnaround in preparing planes for their next flight and offsets some of the inconvenience of travel with humor. They have an efficient route structure as well as a job structure that allows people to share jobs and be very responsive to whatever it takes to get the plane back in the air quickly.

People at Southwest are highly collaborative and flexible. Everybody, from the gate agents to the flight attendants and even the pilots, pitches in to prepare the plane for turnaround. Southwest is able to turn planes around in roughly half the time of many other airlines.

Additionally, Southwest is the only airline that has made money every year for the past five years in the turbulent airline industry. Its strategy has always been to provide low-cost, point-to-point travel in a

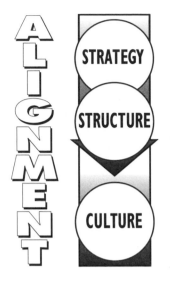

Figure 14.1 © 2006 Senn-Delaney Leadership Consulting Group, LLC.

way that is appealing to customers. The key to doing that is embedded in the culture.

The low-cost message is further communicated in the culture through practices like the shorts and polo shirts worn by flight attendants in the warmer months, and the fun they have with the fact that people "fly for peanuts." Their values, which correspond very closely to the Essential Value Set, focus on accountability through ownership and commitment, healthy state of mind through their positive attitudes, collaboration through teamwork, and flexibility and agility in dealing with change.

In many ways, you could say that culture is Southwest's main strategy. As former CEO Herb Kelleher has said, "we market ourselves based on the personality and spirit of Southwest."

The Secret to Their Success

If you examine their practices, it's apparent that Southwest uses their own form of DURAM™ to systematically create and sustain their culture. People are carefully selected and oriented to fit their brand and constant reinforcement takes place. The flight attendants, customer service reps and baggage handlers are encouraged to take whatever action they feel is appropriate to meet customer needs or help fellow workers, even if that means breaking company policies. When employees make mistakes in judgment, they are rarely punished, but instead are given feedback and coaching on how to improve next time. There is even a tradition of celebrating errors with the intent of turning those lessons into personal growth lessons. All of these cultural practices reinforce the self-worth of employees.

There is a strong emphasis on what we would call organizational health or people's state of mind. A portion of Southwest Airlines' mission statement states that customer service will be "delivered with a sense of warmth, friendliness, individual pride and company spirit."

Southwest's culture is a shadow of its leader, former CEO Kelleher. He is famous for his humorous and eccentric behavior. He has rolled up on his Harley at 2:00 a.m. to host parties for mechanics working the night shift. He has worn costumes and sung rap songs at company events. He has served beverages and handed out snacks to passengers alongside flight attendants. At the same time, he's been a hard-working, results-focused leader. As a result, the culture is an interesting blend, in which people take their jobs very seriously, but don't take themselves too seriously. This leads to a light-hearted spirit and comfortable informality that is directly translated into the customer experience.

Both United and Delta have tried to copy Southwest's successful strategy by creating lower-priced sub-brands. United tried it with both Shuttle by United and Ted. Delta tried with Song. Both used similar aircraft, created similar route structures in high-traffic areas and set competitive fares. To date, neither has succeeded. More than one business journal has observed that they can copy everything, except the culture.

A Different Kind of High-Performance Culture

General Electric (GE) is a very different kind of company, but one where the culture was clearly created to support their strategy of being number one in each of their chosen industry segments. While many people, including the authors, consider the culture a bit harsh, it does drive performance. Jack Welch acknowledged in an interview with us that one of his early mistakes was underestimating the culture and not having a systematic process to shape it. That's what led to the establishment of the John F. Welch Leadership Center at Crotonville in Ossining, New York.

GE followed a form of the DURAM™ change model too. Welch's "diagnosis" was that the former culture tolerated mediocrity and didn't have high-enough expectations. He believed they had to set the bar almost impossibly high to break people of the habit of accepting incremental improvement and look for breakthrough improvement instead. "For example," he explains, "how do you get to ten when you are now at three? We believe you should compare yourself to the best, set the bar at ten, and then have a culture that says if you get to six, you won't be punished. Unfortunately, if a leader sets the bar at four and people get there, he or she has defined their limits."[38]

Welch also defined the kind of culture he wanted by what he called

GE's Leaders Values. It is easy to see the strong performance orientation in those values, which included statements like:

- Understand accountability and commitment and are decisive.

- Set and meet aggressive targets.

- Have a passion for excellence.

- Stimulate and relish change.[39]

The unfreezing/education element of GE's culture shaping took place when leaders and their teams went through the famous "workout" training sessions at Crotonville.

Reinforcement occurred in many ways. Welch was a great believer in personal feedback through the 360° feedback process. He also created a distinctive performance-management process. He became increasingly unhappy with managers' tendency to rate everyone as "OK" or better, which led to the controversial policy of requiring managers to dismiss the lowest-performing 10% of their staff. While we don't tend to believe in such a rigid process, it has sent a strong cultural message at GE.

The result is a culture that supports the strategy of being the best in its industry. It's a high-performance culture, but not necessarily a healthy culture. What you don't see in GE's leaders' values are words like trust, respect, support, or caring.

Welch's successor, Jeffrey Immelt, is making some important shifts in strategy and wisely recognizes that he will also have to shift the culture to make it work. A Business Week article entitled "The Immelt Revolution" states that "he's turning GE's culture upside down." While Welch's focus was to "acquire and make very efficient," Immelt seeks a focus on added organic top-line sales growth through more emphasis on new ideas, customer satisfaction and sales. The article says that Immelt is "worried that GE's famous obsession with bottom-line results—and a tendency to get rid of those that miss them—will make some executives shy away from taking risks that could revolutionize the company."[40]

This is a great example of how a leader can tie culture to strategies and business applications and how new strategies require shifts in culture.

Examples of Organizational Applications

There are many organizations where winning cultures drive strong business results. Here are three examples of clients who have leveraged their culture as a competitive advantage:

The QVC Difference

QVC is the leading television retailer, broadcasting to over 140 million consumers in four major countries. When Doug Briggs took over as CEO from Barry Diller, he wanted to create a culture that captured the essence of QVC's special qualities. Because QVC had been a pioneer in the field, Doug and the senior team selected "Pioneering Spirit" as one of the values. They wanted to promote that pioneering spirit as they searched for different products to bring to their consumers. Another one of QVC's goals was to be a warm, friendly presence in customers' homes. As a result, they selected values that reflected that friendly, service-oriented quality.

They used culture workshops and town-hall-type employee meetings, led by the CEO and senior team members, to take the values to all parts and all levels of the organization. The spirit of the values is called "The QVC Difference." As Doug says, "*The QVC Difference* is making a difference in who we are as a company and what we are able to achieve. It's helping us every day in how we do things."[41]

The pioneering spirit shows up in their 50-state tour to find the most innovative new ideas for products. The friendly, neighborly value is evident in dealing with QVC employees, from the show hosts to staff at some of the most personal and service-oriented call centers in the world. The culture has made a difference at QVC, and it has been applied in QVC's own unique way with The QVC Difference.

United Stationers and the War on Waste

At $4.3 billion in sales, United Stationers is North America's largest broad-line wholesale distributor of business products. They provide technology products, traditional business products, office furniture items, janitorial and sanitation products, and food service consumables to resellers. When Richard Gochnauer took over as president and CEO, he saw profit potential in creating a more efficient organization. One means to achieving that was to establish high-performance teams throughout the organization and focus them on what he called "the war on waste."

The senior teams created a new set of values that defined both the desired culture and the behaviors for all high-performance teams. They worked to create productive meeting dynamics and ways for the teams to measure results. Geographic teams, sales teams, product teams, distribution center teams and merchandising teams all took part in high-performance team trainings.

United Stationer's team-based "war" has saved more than $20 million annually in costs for three consecutive years, and their stock price doubled during that same time period. For those who think winning teams and winning cultures are "soft" topics, the results at United Stationers prove otherwise.

STAPLES: THAT WAS EASY

Staples founded the office superstore concept in 1986 and soon faced competition from some twenty other start-ups. Extensive market research in 2002 revealed a potential competitive advantage if Staples could simplify the shopping experience and make it easy for customers to buy what they needed. The "Easy Brand" promise was unveiled in 2003 and it has had a dramatic impact on the company's performance.

In the early stages of development, it became clear that to successfully execute this strategy required a transformation of Staples' culture. It had long been task-driven and focused on being "cheap and complete." While prices were low and the offering plentiful, shopping at Staples was an undifferentiated experience.

To shape the culture, the executive team held a series of workshops to fully understand the existing culture and define the qualities needed to support the Easy Brand promise. They decided to build the "Easy" culture around a new set of values, called TeamCARE, a term which captured the inspirational principles of Teamwork together with a focus on the Customer, Associates, Results and Easy. The executives made personal commitments to live these principles and encouraged their associates to become "brand advocates" as well. Regular formal and informal reinforcements keep the principles vibrant. Results have been impressive. An annual comprehensive survey of all associates monitors the state of the culture. From the 2002 baseline, cultural results have improved every year. The promise of competitive advantage has been realized, and today Staples is the world's leading seller of office products.

COLLABORATING FOR THE CUSTOMER

We have worked with several regional banks who have decided they can best compete with the larger national banks by becoming "trusted business advisors" to the people and communities they serve. That strategy requires a culture that is more personal, friendly, and highly collaborative in order to bring together all the products necessary to satisfy a customer. Bank of Hawaii has significantly improved their financial strength and profitability and moved up in the rankings of banks their size by executing a strategy that makes them the best at "serving their island communities."

Another bank working on their culture to pursue that strategy is KeyBank. They conducted extensive research on customer needs and determined that becoming a trusted business advisor required higher levels of cross-functional collaboration between their divisions.

Their culture, like most, was one of independent silos, each serving its own specific customer set. They undertook a corporate-wide initiative called the Customer Experience Process (CEP) with significant investments in IT, new processes, product development and employee training. In order for CEP to succeed, however, the culture needed to change to one of collaboration, trust, accountability for the greater team success, embracing change, and operating from an open, healthy state of mind.

During the diagnostic phase, data from KeyBank's Corporate Culture Profile™ identified the cultural qualities they needed to change most in order to best support their "trusted advisor" strategy. Their culture-shaping process was called "*I AM KEY.*" The senior team launched it to all levels of management, preceded by a company-wide communication plan to build the case for change.

As they introduced the new initiatives—including a new organization-wide CRM system—senior leaders and managers all used the new

"*I AM KEY*" language and concepts to help them implement their changes. Team leaders continued to focus on the new "*I AM KEY*" values in staff and cross-functional meetings, and a process was established to measure divisional and departmental progress. Leaders were encouraged to "walk the talk" in their project meetings and in all employee interactions.

With the powerful shadow cast by the senior leadership and management, "*I AM KEY*" became the new "rules of the road," and took KeyBank a long way toward supporting the CEP initiative, which was critical to their success.

Organizational Structure

In addition to strategy, another company-wide application of culture is in the area of organizational structure, or the organizational model. One factor that has caused companies to conclude they needed to work on their culture is a desire to gain more cross-organizational synergies. Most larger companies have separate major business units, either through design or acquisition. The question for these organizations is, can the whole be greater than the sum of its parts? How can we leverage those synergies that exist between businesses?

Many companies now realize they need to move from a holding-company model to more of a shared- or allied-business model. One reason for the desire to implement shared services better is to be more cost-effective. Another strong influence is the voice of the customer. Customers today are looking for solutions vs. products, and organizations can provide solutions only when different parts of the organization are able to work together in presenting one face to the customer.

There are some historic, as well as, current examples of the need to shift culture in order to shift structure. Bell Atlantic, as we've cited earlier, is a classic example. Their need to move from a monopolistic holding-company format with largely autonomous state phone companies to a more agile, global competitor could never be done with the we-they issues and silos that existed between the phone companies. The key to the cultural shift was creating a set of attitudes and behaviors based on collaborating and making decisions for the greater good.

Another example of culture supporting a shift in organizational model is the dramatic improvement in financial performance at

Nationwide. The progress was a result of moving from a holding company to an allied-business model.

At a senior team culture-shaping seminar with the three major Nationwide business units and their teams, Jerry Jurgensen, the new CEO, drew three circles on a flip chart, representing the three separate business units. In the diagram, Jerry showed the circles not totally separated, but with an area of overlap. He then told the group that their collective goal was to find opportunities in that area of overlap. The session worked on the behaviors, such as trust and collaboration, they needed to achieve that goal.

As the senior leadership and the organization under them started to live the new values and apply them to the shared model, they found more opportunities for shared services and joint business solutions. Each leader and his or her team worked to apply the Nationwide values to the shared-service projects. The values were featured in company publications, leaders used them at cross-functional meetings, and periodic measurements were taken to assess their implementation. As different units in the holding company began to share both resources and customer information, financial improvements in both cost savings and revenue resulted.

Hundreds of organizations today are moving toward shared-business models. Their level of success depends largely on their cultures, because cultures either facilitate or defeat such shifts.

Acquisitions

Companies that are the most successful at acquiring other firms have a clearly defined, healthy, high-performance culture themselves. In the case of large mergers, avoiding cultural clash requires that organizations understand both their own culture and that of the company with whom they are merging. The Anthem/WellPoint Health Networks merger is an example of a successful merger of equals. Larry Glasscock, the CEO of the acquiring organization Anthem, was tuned in to the importance of the culture from the beginning. He took the time to build the new combined team and to involve them in defining and leading the cultural integration. As a result, the merger exceeded all targets set.

When larger companies acquire smaller ones they often assimilate them, or absorb them into the parent organization. In other cases, the acquired company becomes a "bolt-on" that operates with semi-autonomy but still needs to connect to the parent organization to gain the synergies and add value. In either case, this is easier to do when the acquiring company has a culture that is attractive for people to live in and connect to.

Meeting the Numbers

One client was facing financial challenges as a part of a leveraged buyout (LBO). They had to meet their numbers for the year to satisfy bank requirements at a time when their industry was in a slump. As a part of their culture-shaping effort, the senior team signed up to:

- Develop a greater bias for action

- Focus on contributing to the corporate win, not their own divisional success at the corporation's expense

- Hold themselves, each other and their direct reports even more accountable for reaching the numbers with a can-do, "no excuses" attitude

- Become better coaches and be open to coaching

At each meeting and group discussion they attended, the senior team members communicated and demonstrated by word and deed their commitment to lead with the values and cast a powerful shadow throughout the organization. As they, and their teams, lived the values, they exceeded their required financial performance.

Making Lean Manufacturing Work

Manufacturing firms in Europe and North America are constantly being pushed to become more efficient, so they can compete more effectively. Most manufacturers have moved toward a manufacturing model that incorporates many features of the "lean production system" first developed by Toyota many years ago.

Many companies have adopted the process and yet have not yielded the results they expected. What is not as apparent in the Toyota Production system is the culture that drives it. The attitudes and behaviors of the people are what make the system work. Lean manufacturing requires high levels of teamwork, decisions for the greater good and empowerment in the sense that people continuously contribute improvement ideas and are wiling to stop the line for quality issues when required. Those things have always been in place at Toyota, but not necessarily at other companies that use versions of their lean manufacturing system.

Airbus, like many manufacturing firms, initiated a performance-improvement program using the tools of Six Sigma and lean manufacturing. Although they achieved some level of performance improvement, VP of Operations Phil Swash observed, "Things just weren't sticking because not everyone was participating."

Swash felt that his employees' attitudes were limiting the program's potential. "Quite frankly they just didn't want to be engaged." Lean manufacturing tools, techniques and processes seemed to be providing only a part of the solution. There must be a missing piece. But what was it?

This missing component was to develop leadership behaviors and break down silos—in short, to align the culture of the organization with its business objectives. By doing so, Airbus would be able to realize gains far beyond those it could achieve through lean-manufacturing techniques alone. Swash commented, "The culture-shaping process made it considerably easier to implement the manufacturing tools."

"We wanted to avoid the sheep-dip phenomenon in which managers are dunked in a pleasant hot bath of training but quickly revert back to their old behaviors. The classroom training, while excellently facilitated, was only one component of the overall systems approach for aligning everyone, from senior management to hourly workers, with our business objectives," says Swash.

Airbus reinforced the classroom experience through a series of mini-surveys implemented every three months. By targeting the smaller business units, they were able to compile metrics on how the culture-shaping initiative was helping to move the needle in a positive and tangible direction.

As Swash commented, "Many manufacturing leaders spend countless years wishing for a change in culture, but avoid doing anything about it because they don't know where to start...or because they see it as a soft option. My learning is that...it starts with me and my team and it is anything but the soft option."

And the bottom-line results? According to Swash, "This year we will achieve about a 14% productivity improvement, which is about three times what we have achieved before. It greatly exceeds the industry norm of between one and five percent per annum. Absenteeism rates have fallen from about 7% to about 3%, which, in a plant of the size of ours, has a significant impact on productivity and performance."

THE ROLE OF CULTURE IN BUILDING THE BRAND

On more than one occasion, advertising agencies and branding firms have said to us, "It would be great if the firms we represent could actually be what we advertise them to be." All too often, branding initiatives are designed for external public perception, but are little more than advertising campaigns. As most branding executives know, a company's distinctive brand includes the interaction and experience customers have with the employees of the company.

Senn-Delaney Leadership's earliest culture shaping work was on customer service in retailing, and it was obvious to us that culture is a great way to "*be* the brand." Retailers could see in companies like Nordstrom that service was a cultural phenomenon, not a "program." Nordstrom has created a brand around superior service, which translates to "we are easy to do business with." They can only execute this as long as each Nordstrom employee "lives" this brand promise with each customer contact as well as with each other internally.

The brand can mean many things, even in retailing. Neil Fiske and Ken Stevens, the co-leaders of Bath and Body Works, one of the Limited Brands, knew this as they embarked upon a major brand shift. Bath and Body Works was viewed historically as more of a country store. The new vision was to be the "modern apothecary of beauty and well-being." Aspects of this new vision included product changes, such as new well-being products, a new look in the stores and many other elements. Historically, this is where most such branding initiatives would stop.

Fiske, Stevens and their senior team saw the wisdom of shifting the culture to ensure that the shadow cast by leadership, and the behavior of store associates, was consistent with the new brand. If the store were to represent *well-being*, then the style of leadership and the way customers were served also needed to represent well-being. The senior team latched onto the Mood Elevator from their leadership, team-building and culture-shaping process as a symbol of the change. As a result, the organization worked simultaneously on the strategy, the structure (including product, presentation and promotion), and the culture to support all of that. From a cultural standpoint, the higher states of the Mood Elevator were symbolic of the feeling they wanted for customers in the stores. Because the language of the new culture was broadly used, there was a common understanding of what *well-being* in the stores represented.

The Bath and Body Works success story is a great example of a more holistic approach to dealing with strategy, brand, process, leadership and culture simultaneously.

culture shaping is most effective when applied to real-life business initiatives. Application of learning helps anchor it and create new thought patterns and habits, as well as, new individual, team and organizational behaviors. When it comes to culture shaping, the old adage "use it or lose it" applies. "Use it" in this context means apply your cultural values explicitly and very publicly to real-life organization initiatives. When the results occur, celebrate your culture for the role it played. In that way, you can take culture from the soft category of "nice to have" to the solid category of "must have."

QUESTIONS TO CONSIDER

1. What organization-wide strategies, changes or initiatives would a high-performance culture help support in your organization?

   _____

   _____

   _____

   _____

   _____

2. What elements in your culture would need to change to best support the success of those initiatives?

   _____

   _____

   _____

   _____

   _____

HOW DO WE KNOW IT'S WORKING?
MEASUREMENT GIVES YOU THE ANSWER.

Figure 15.1 © 2006 Senn-Delaney Leadership Consulting Group, LLC.

"What gets measured gets people's attention!"

— Anonymous

Establishing values and communicating about them is useful, but unless individuals, teams and organizations are measured on progress, culture shaping is less likely to occur. Measurement is the accountability element in culture shaping. When used correctly, it can answer questions like:

- Are teams performing better?

- Is our culture shifting?

- Is the change impacting results?

JIM: Measurement gets our attention—at work, and in all walks of life. Let me share a personal example: after a particularly frustrating round of golf one day, I decided to go to a local pro and take a lesson to improve my game.

What this golf pro did for me is what all consultants and coaches should do for leaders. First, he **diagnosed** my stance, grip, and swing; and then he helped **unfreeze** my old habits and educated me on a new stance and swing. After the lesson, he sent me to the driving range to **reinforce** what I had learned. Finally after hitting many buckets of balls at distance signs, it was time for me to **apply** what I had learned on the course. He then told me to **measure** and monitor my progress in a variety of ways.

So, during my next round of golf, I measured my results in several ways including my score (which actually went up due to trying many new things). I also measured the number of fairways hit, number of greens hit in regulation, and number of putts. These measurements allowed me to see my progress in each aspect of my game and to focus on key areas for improvement. After a few months of reinforcement, application and measurement, my scores did improve.

The lesson here is that while learning a new golf stance and swing would be interesting, the improvement would not have taken place without practice (applying the lessons) and measurement of results. The same could be said when it comes to culture shaping: "If you can't measure it, you can't be sure it changed."

In the business world, plans and strategies are great but in the end, success is measured by results. Senn-Delaney Leadership has always been clear about that, as stated in our mission: "We help leaders create healthy, high-performance cultures *to consistently achieve better results.*"

MEASURING ORGANIZATIONAL CULTURE

Since culture-change processes are designed to operate at three levels, measurement should also take place at the same three levels to ensure change occurs. They are:

- The individual level, in terms of his/her behaviors

- The team level, in terms of interpersonal dynamics

- The organizational level, in terms of cultural values, behaviors and results

Companies don't often directly measure their "culture." They may measure employee attitudes, or, at best, employee engagement, but do they know if they have the healthy, high-performance behaviors needed to maximize results? Few do. Special tools and measures are needed to support a culture shaping effort.

For years, companies have been attempting to measure the attitude of employees (and, by inference, the overall corporation) through the use of morale and opinion surveys. While these have had some value in recording how people feel about issues like benefits, supervision, management, service levels and quality, as a whole they have been ineffective in providing insight into how to improve employee engagement and overall corporate performance. One of the failings of these attitude surveys is that they often depend upon the feeling at the moment, and thus are subject to the normal ups and downs of human personality, quarterly performance and the latest event on people's minds.

The results of opinion surveys can change with the announcement of a restructuring or during a difficult labor negotiation. What is really being measured is how people feel about things, not how well individuals and teams are functioning in getting their jobs done. While feelings are interesting, they do not give us insight into the root causes of performance shortfalls or customer problems.

We believe that traditional attitude surveys are part of the old business paradigm. They are in part a holdover from the unwritten contract that companies had with employees in past decades:

"We'll take care of you and provide for your security, and you give us your dedication and loyalty."

Since high-performance behaviors and high-performance teams create results for organizations, it is more important to ask about things like levels of cross-organizational teamwork than about how people feel. If you want to know if you are moving toward a high-performance culture, it is more important to know that there is a bias for action and a can-do attitude than it is to know how unhappy people are about declining medical benefits.

A whole new approach to measuring and monitoring organizational and individual performance is needed to provide today's corporations with a more effective set of performance-improvement tools. Instead of seeking to measure attitudes, we recommend measuring high-performance values and behaviors. When it comes to evaluating the strength of the culture shaping, you need to know how well you are doing relative to the *behaviors that define the desired culture.*

The Corporate Culture Profile™, described in Chapter 6, is designed to do just that. It measures a series of behaviors that impact bottom-line performance, employee engagement and customer focus. Done at the start of a culture-shaping initiative, it provides a baseline. When it is repeated, it lets an organization know how well they are doing in changing behaviors.

Early on, the new CEO of a Fortune 100 financial services firm decided that a shift in culture was needed to improve performance, and to support the changes being made in shifting from a holding company to a shared-business model. At the start of a culture-shaping initiative, the CEO and his senior team articulated the behaviors they needed to make that happen. The Corporate Culture Profile™ below (Figure 15.2) captured the transformational change that took place. The changes in many of the cultural behaviors were dramatic. Three of the greatest improvements were in behaviors the CEO set out to change— increased accountability, added bias for action and cross-organizational teamwork.

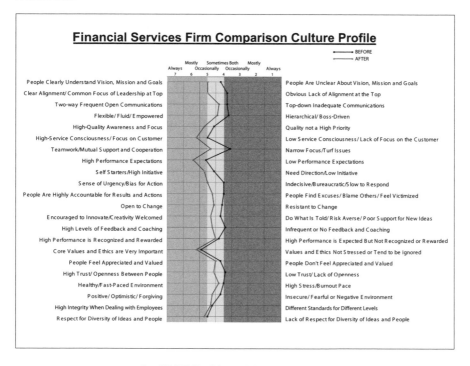

Figure 15.2 © 2006 Senn-Delaney Leadership Consulting Group, LLC.

The company had a commensurate increase in profitability, return on investment and economic value.

The cultural profile can be used in a variety of ways, including:

- Determining how deeply cultural habits are embedded in the organization

- Determining subtle cultural differences when global organizations introduce cross-country initiatives

- Highlighting the potential of a "culture clash" between organizations involved in mergers and acquisitions

MEASURING TEAMS

The same questions in the Corporate Culture Profile™ can be used to create a Team Profile. Since it is very simple to repeat the measure, the team can check on its progress every six months and use the data to refocus on areas needing further improvement. Below (Figure 15.3) is an example of one team's profile prior to a leadership and culture-shaping process and then again six months later.

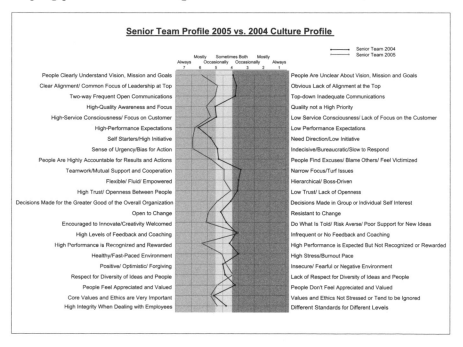

Figure 15.3 © 2006 Senn-Delaney Leadership Consulting Group, LLC.

Each zone is based on normative data and also based on use by thousands of teams. The traits of the team fall into one of the three zones: 1) scores below 4.0 are in red, for danger; 2) yellow means caution; 3) green, at 5.0 and above, is healthy, high-performance.

Measurement of the senior team is critical. The complaint in most companies is that the senior team isn't walking the talk. The team profile makes them more aware of, and accountable for, the shadow they cast. For instance, if an organization is implementing a shared services initiative, and the senior leadership team scores low on collaboration and trust, they are not likely to succeed in that initiative.

The shadow phenomenon is so powerful that once we have the profile for the senior team we generally have the pattern of the profile for the rest of the organization. While there are some differences, the highest and lowest scores for the senior team are often the highest and lowest scores for the company.

Individual Measurement

Cultural change requires personal change.

In a sense, you don't change cultures, you shift the behaviors of individuals *in* the culture. Behavior change needs to take place from the CEO on down. If change is taking place, it is observable and therefore it is measurable.

Many organizations have or have used instruments to measure leaders behaviors based on the perception of those that work with the leaders. They usually take the form of 360° (multirater) feedback from peers, direct reports and a boss. Such instruments are useful because they help us see ourselves as others experience us. They increase our self-awareness and overcome our blind spots. Finally, they let us know if we are making progress or not.

> *"O wad some power the giftie give us to see oursel's as others see us."*
>
> *—Robert Burns*

Traditional 360° Do's and Don'ts

Unfortunately, many 360° processes are not developed, utilized or administered in a way which gains employee acceptance or best promotes the desired culture shaping. To be most effective, the following common errors need to be avoided:

- Don't use a generic or "off-the-shelf" 360° survey.

Many companies use standard or generic 360° surveys. They can be helpful in coaching people on behaviors but we have found these to be ineffective in shaping a culture. If the culture has been defined in terms of behaviors A, B and C, and the 360° measures behaviors D, E and F, the feedback is not nearly as useful.

Ideally, the 360° inventory is totally customized—based upon the organization's own defined values and guiding behaviors. If teamwork has been defined by five guiding-behavior statements, then those same five statements should be used to define teamwork in the 360°. In that way, the 360° can show how each person is living the values and guiding behaviors of the new culture.

- Do start the 360° process with Senior Management.

The 360° inventory should be developed and used first by the senior team, including the CEO. This group casts the longest shadow— if they are not effectively role-modeling the elements and behaviors of the new culture, neither will the rest of the organization.

When the senior team completes their 360° feedback inventory and openly discuss it with their direct reports they create the right atmosphere for change to occur in the culture. It is a sign of added openness and trust and it increases the readiness of the next levels to take part in this process themselves.

- Don't introduce the 360° process in ways that are threatening to people.

People like data on performance so long as it is for their eyes only and they can control who sees it. Therefore, it is generally a mistake to make it available to a person's boss or use it for compensation. It is a development tool. Introduced as such, the 360° can be very well received. People do rely on measurement in many day-to-day activities, such as dieting, family budgeting, golf scoring, sports ladder standings, health measures, and exercise schedules. We, as critical-thinking human beings, have always rated and will always rate ourselves to see how we are doing from one day to another, in almost any walk of life. Who doesn't have a weight scale in their house?

As long as the results from these measurements are kept private (i.e., how many people know how much you weigh?) and shared at the discretion of the owner of the results, most people view these measures as informative and productive. Once the private results of these measures are made public, the measures go from personally motivating to somewhat intimidating.

We find that the 360° process is readily embraced when utilized in the following format:

- It corresponds with how the culture has been defined according to the values and guiding behaviors of the organization.

- It is administered after people have personal exposure to the cultural values in a culture-change seminar. (They are then more open to self development and more curious about themselves.)

- Confidentiality is ensured by giving the participants a great deal of control over the instrument, by allowing them to distribute the 360° surveys themselves and receive the findings back without others in the company having access to their results.

- The 360° process begins with the senior team and then moves down in the organization.

The "Living the Values" or "Guiding Behaviors" Inventory

Senn-Delaney Leadership has developed an instrument that meets the criteria in the 360° do and don't list. We generally refer to it as a Guiding Behaviors Inventory™ while some clients call it a **Living the Values Inventory™**. It plays an important role in the DURAM™ change model by closing the loop from the **D** for definition to the **M** for measurement. It does so by fully aligning the questions in the inventory with the values and behaviors that define the culture. Most organizations have stated values. What they may not have is specific observable behaviors that indicate whether or not a person is living that value. Values need descriptors or "guiding behaviors" that each leader will be trained in, signed up for and measured on. For instance, an organization could select a value like "accountability." The question is, what do we mean by that and how might we measure leaders on living that value? The answer is to define behaviors that describe accountable behavior, such as "Has a can-do attitude" and "Persists through obstacles to achieve results." Teamwork may be a value but if you need cross-organizational collaboration you may need a behavior to describe it such as, "Makes decisions for the greater good, not self interest."

Generally there are four to six guiding behaviors that define each value for an organization. These guiding behaviors can be put together in a Guiding Behaviors Inventory™ (GBI) to help people understand their specific strengths and challenges.

Benefits of 360° Feedback Inventory

- A useful snapshot of how the individual is seen to be living the organization's Shared Values and Guiding Behaviors.
- A non-threatening and confidential mechanism for team members and associates to give each other developmental feedback.
- A useful road map for improvement.
- Increased awareness of leadership abilities and team behavior through precise feedback from the manager, peers, direct reports, and customers.
- A vehicle for effective coaching.

Figure 15.4 © 2006 Senn-Delaney Leadership Consulting Group, LLC.

If organized in this format and presented in a non-threatening manner, the GBI can be a powerful developmental tool. We find the best information comes from having a recipient of the data look at the highest-scoring five to ten behaviors and the lowest-scoring five to ten behaviors and then reading the written comments. A "story" almost always emerges that sounds like, "I do very well at these kinds of things and should leverage that strength; and it is clear that the general area for me to work on is the following."

A sample of answers for one value is shown on the next page, together with a list of the top ten and bottom ten scores (Figures 15.5-15.7). If this were a sample of your data, what would you make of it?

Sample Participant | Collaboration Value—We Partner with Each Other

This section shows your respondents' perceptions of how consistently you display these behaviors. The scores shown are averages of all respondents in each relationship category. In all categories except "Self" and "Manager", at least 2 responses were required in order for the category to be displayed. (Note: the "All Responses" score does not include "Self" rating.)

7. Values, respects and is open to the points of view of others and seeks the wisdom of the team to meet SDL and Client needs.

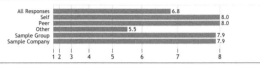

8. Seeks to understand client needs and partners to provide satisfying solutions to those needs.

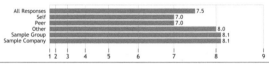

9. Is unselfish in seeking the best outcomes rather than those that benefit him/her most.

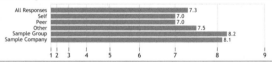

10. Partners by developing open, trusting, respectful working relationships and a team spirit with clients and teammates.

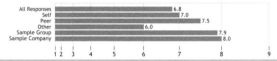

Figure 15.5 © 2006 Senn-Delaney Leadership Consulting Group, LLC.

Sample Participant | Top 10 Strengths

This section is based on an average of the "all respondents" score for each behavior (see Personal Data section). The top 10 results are ranked in order from highest to lowest. You will get greater value from this data by looking for themes rather than focusing on the actual numerical scores.

↑ above company average

→ *company average*

↓ below company average

Average Score	Behavior*		Value
8.8	Asks "what more can I or we do" to help move projects, processes or client engagements forward to the next step. (19)	↑	Accountability
8.5	Can be counted on to keep agreements. (33)	↑	Integrity
8.3	Takes ownership for results with a "can do" attitude and a healthy "sense of urgency." (20)	↑	Accountability
8.0	Minimizes issues and agendas by speaking directly with the right individual, not others; i.e., does not contribute to triangles, rumors and hidden agendas. (29)	↑	Communication
8.0	Is resourceful, and innovative in overcoming obstacles and finding solutions. (22)	↑	Accountability
8.0	Is accountable to ensure that clients achieve their desired goals. (23)	↓	Accountability
8.0	Contributes to a positive, light (fun) and purposeful environment. (4)	↑	Health
8.0	Is personally accountable to continuously gain the knowledge and skills about business, products and processes needed to better serve clients and SDL. (15)	↑	Change
7.8	Maintains perspective with a hopeful, confident and optimistic attitude, even in the face of challenges and setbacks. (2)	→	Health
7.8	Exhibits insight, wisdom and creativity with ideas and solutions for clients and teammates. (3)	→	Health

* Refers to question number from report to follow

Figure 15.6 © 2006 Senn-Delaney Leadership Consulting Group, LLC.

Sample Participant | Top 10 Challenges

This section is based on an average of the "all respondents" score for each behavior (see Personal Data section). The top 10 results are ranked in order from highest to lowest. You will get greater value from this data by looking for themes rather than focusing on the actual numerical scores.

↑   above company average

→   *company average*

↓   below company average

Average Score	Behavior*		Value
6.0	Takes responsibility for bringing other people and resources into the process in order to achieve a broader win. (11)	↓	Partner
6.0	Coaches with respect and compassion. (27)	↓	Communication
6.3	Actively seeks input and feedback from others, and receives it in an open manner. (13)	↓	Change
6.3	Consistently displays humility, curiosity and openness to learning and change. (14)	↓	Change
6.5	Practices SDL foundational principles of openness to learning via insight and seeking to better understand the role of thought. (35)	↓	Integrity
6.8	Is open and honest and does not withhold information. (34)	↓	Integrity
6.8	Partners by developing open, trusting, respectful working relationships and a team spirit with clients and teammates. (10)	↓	Partner
6.8	Values, respects and is open to the points of view of others and seeks the wisdom of the team to meet SDL and Client needs. (7)	↓	Partner
7.0	Creates open, trusting and respectful relationships. (1)	↓	Health
7.0	Encourages others to express their views, even if contrary. (25)	↓	Communication

* Refers to question number from report to follow

Figure 15.7 © 2006 Senn-Delaney Leadership Consulting Group, LLC.

A Simpler Alternative

As valuable as they are, one of the common complaints about 360° feedback instruments is that they are very time-consuming, because there are so many questions, and they must be completed by so many people. A simple but useful alternative is to have fewer people fill out a survey with fewer questions in an easy-to-use online format.

We have created such an alternative; an abbreviated values inventory that requires just one response on each value. Five values require just five clicks of the mouse. A leader selects five or six peers who can give feedback on how they are leading relative to the values. The tool then consolidates the feedback and ranks the leader from their strongest value to the one that needs the most improvement. Respondents also have an opportunity to enter both appreciative and constructive comments to help guide the leader for future development. All responses are confidential and consolidated to ensure anonymity. (Figure 15.8, on next page)

Values Inventory Profile Executive Review

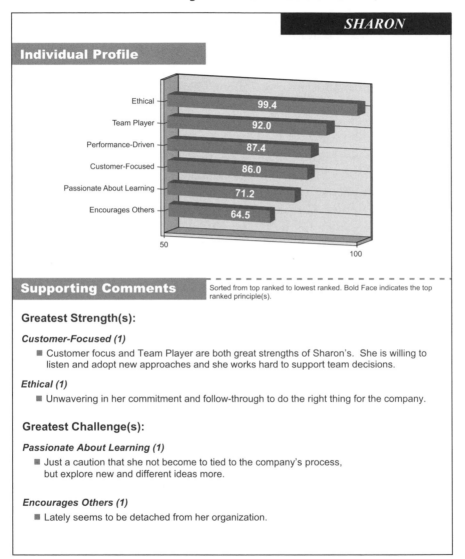

SHARON

Individual Profile

Ethical	99.4
Team Player	92.0
Performance-Driven	87.4
Customer-Focused	86.0
Passionate About Learning	71.2
Encourages Others	64.5

50   100

Supporting Comments

Sorted from top ranked to lowest ranked. Bold Face indicates the top ranked principle(s).

Greatest Strength(s):

Customer-Focused (1)
- Customer focus and Team Player are both great strengths of Sharon's. She is willing to listen and adopt new approaches and she works hard to support team decisions.

Ethical (1)
- Unwavering in her commitment and follow-through to do the right thing for the company.

Greatest Challenge(s):

Passionate About Learning (1)
- Just a caution that she not become to tied to the company's process, but explore new and different ideas more.

Encourages Others (1)
- Lately seems to be detached from her organization.

Figure 15.8 © 2006 Senn-Delaney Leadership Consulting Group, LLC.

This quick assessment instrument can be administered frequently and can help leaders gain an accurate assessment of their progress in casting a healthy, high-performance shadow.

Custom-Designed Organizational Metrics

The measures we have shown earlier in this chapter, such as the Corporate Culture Profile™ and the Guiding Behaviors Inventory™, track behavior changes in individuals, teams and cultures. For example, the results can show whether collaboration or coaching has increased, or if blaming and resistance to change have decreased. Since the goal of culture shaping is to increase performance, some way is needed to better tie behavior change to quantitative metrics on performance.

Systems to measure and link subjective culture shaping and objective bottom-line results need to be custom designed at the outset of a culture-shaping process and measured throughout. Here is an example of how one client did this.

Case Study: A Global Commercial Aircraft Manufacturer

Facing fierce competition, this manufacturer decided that they needed to improve performance in six areas:

- Cost reduction: 5% year-over-year

- Quality improvement: defect reduction of 15% year-over-year

- Customer satisfaction: 100% delivery and satisfaction

- Safety: accident-free environment

- Lean Manufacturing: create a continuous improvement culture

- Employee satisfaction: 5% increase

They calculated that once these goals were achieved, their financial performance would be improved by realizing a *$20 million savings per year for three straight years*. By any standards, these were ambitious goals for the leadership of this manufacturing plant, with over 7,000 unionized employees.

The achievement of the cost reduction goals was largely dependent on doing an even better job with the lean manufacturing principles and accelerating continuous improvement. The measurement question became, what are the human or cultural drivers that will make that happen? We identified a series of motivational drivers from a combination of normative data from other manufacturing environments and focus groups in aircraft manufacturing. The in-plant culture-shaping process, including training and reinforcement, then focused on improving scores in both the Essential Values and the specific Internal Motivators for people. (Figures 15.9 and 15.10)

In just a year's time, having a culture that supports performance showed significant improvement:

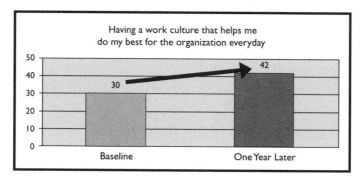

Figure 15.9 © 2006 Senn-Delaney Leadership Consulting Group, LLC.

Huge shifts in behaviors people experience were widely noticable:

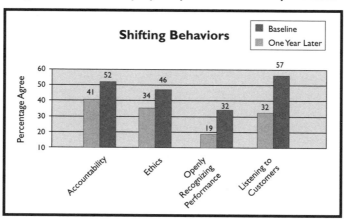

Figure 15.10 © 2006 Senn-Delaney Leadership Consulting Group, LLC.

The plant's senior leadership team was aware that unless they could shape a healthy, high-performance culture in both the management and plant, they would be unable to achieve their goals. They knew they needed to raise alignment levels, accountability, collaboration and openness to change. They also knew they needed to work on the Internal Motivators of appreciating and valuing employees, as well as involvement and empowerment. To ensure they received a return on the culture-shaping initiative, the leadership team tracked the improvement in each of these categories and then tied it to their performance goals.

One year into the process, they observed significant movement in each behavioral category and were exceeding all of their objective goals of quality improvement, cost reduction, employee satisfaction, on-time deliveries, and accident-free environment. As a result they were able to exceed the targeted $20 million in annual savings.

QUESTIONS TO CONSIDER

1. Do we have a measurement system for our culture?

_____

_____

2. Are we measuring at all three levels: individual, team and organization?

_____

_____

3. Is our 360° process, if we have one, tied directly to the behaviors
   that define our culture?

_____

_____

4. Do our behavioral metrics tie directly to achieving our business
   objectives?

_____

_____

16

VISION AND THE HIGH-PERFORMANCE PYRAMID

The connection between business results and a healthy culture is not always clear to everyone. We have helped many clients better communicate that connection to the entire organization using a customized graphic model we call a High-Performance Pyramid.

After Bank of Hawaii's senior team aligned around their vision, mission and strategic imperatives, they created a high-performance pyramid that illustrated the relationship between their vision, strategy and culture to communicate these messages to the organization (Figure 16.1). The CEO used the pyramid in discussions with employees, in meetings, in the annual report, and even created desktop pyramids for all employees throughout the organization.

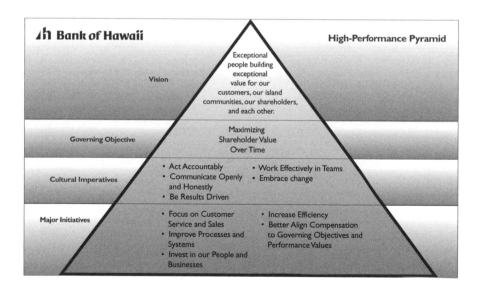

Figure 16.1 Bank of Hawaii. Used with permission (2006).

The process of creating the pyramid aligned the senior team and provided a vehicle to discuss the culture and its importance. It also helped Bank of Hawaii execute strategies that significantly improved their performance.

Because each organization's vision, strategies and culture is different, each pyramid is unique. Typically, it includes the vision or mission at the top, the strategic imperatives in the middle, and the values that define the desired culture at the base.

Peter Darbee, CEO of Pacific Gas and Electric (PG&E), and his senior team developed the pyramid below (Figure 16.2) as they set their new direction in the wake of the recent California energy crisis.

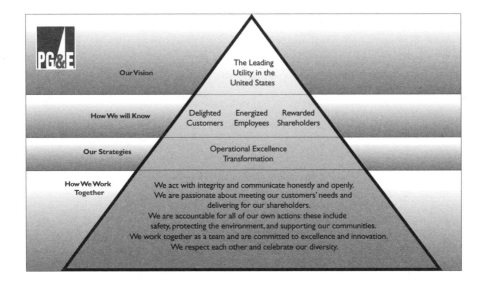

Figure 16.2 Pacific Gas & Electric. Used with permission (2006).

Each of the elements in the pyramid plays an important role. One useful metaphor is a bicycle and how it gets to its destination. The front wheel—like vision, mission and strategy—directs the bicycle along the right path. The rear wheel (and the rider), like the culture, provides the power for forward movement. Likewise, high-performance organizations combine a compelling vision of the future, a clear set of strategies and a high-performance culture to achieve its goals.

Vision: The Directional Principle for Purpose and Meaning

At the top of the high-performance pyramid is *vision*. A well-stated vision for an organization plays the same role that a life purpose does for an individual: both are motivational and directional. For an individual, purpose often takes the form of providing or caring for family, commitment to a religious faith, being the best at something or making a positive difference in the community or in the world. For an organization, purpose or vision provides the reason for existence.

> *"Where there is no vision, the people will perish."*
> —*Proverbs 29:18*

While values and guiding behaviors describe how people operate, vision provides the fuel, motivation and energy needed to win in a competitive marketplace.

> *"Vision is extremely valuable for rallying the spirit, feeling and commitment of our people."*
> —*John Pepper*
> *Former Chairman, Procter & Gamble*[42]

Vision is the magnetic force that unleashes the drive, energy, creativity and courage needed to reach an objective. Compelling visions have empowered and released human and organizational potential throughout history. The powerful vision of a land where people were equal and able to control their own destinies allowed the fledgling American colony to wrest freedom from the much larger and better-financed British crown.

In many ways, a clear vision represents "magnetic north" for employees within a high-performance organization. It also represents the idealized picture of what the company and its employees can become. A vision is much more than just a goal or picture of a future; it evokes a strong feeling. It is the feeling, not the goal, which inspires high energy and commitment.

Empowered employees, but no clear vision

- -

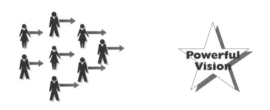

Empowered employees; clear, powerful vision

Figure 16.3 © 2006 Senn-Delaney Leadership Consulting Group, LLC.

In our work, we have found there are a limited number of universal themes that resonate with most people by striking a cord deep within them:

1. Improving the Quality of Life

For example, Microsoft's Bill Gates, stated that his vision is "to put a PC on everyone's desk." This vision, when achieved, can make people more effective and improve their lives.

2. Serving Others

An organization might realize this vision by having the best service or providing the best value.

3. Winning, Being the Best or Being Part of an Excellent Team

People will mobilize around a vision that calls for being the best at what they do.

4. Making a Difference

Most people have a deep-seated need to feel that what they do makes a difference. Our vision at Senn-Delaney Leadership falls under this category: *We are a healthy, high-performance team committed to making a difference in the spirit and performance of organizations.*

Not all companies have both a vision and a mission; some combine the two. If there is a distinction, it is that the role of a vision is to motivate and inspire, while the mission clarifies what the organization excels in. For example, our mission is to "create healthy, high-performance cultures that improve business results." While our vision captures people's desire to make a difference, the mission better clarifies the business we are in; that is, shaping organizational cultures to help clients enhance business results.

Figure 16.4 © 2006 Senn-Delaney Leadership Consulting Group, LLC.

The Foundation of the Pyramid

The base of the pyramid should be the organization's values. In the figure on the previous page (Figure 16.4), we have represented these as Senn-Delaney Leadership's version of the Essential Values with the performance value, or accountability, at the top and the organizational health value as the base.

In order to build a great culture, each person needs to strive to lead and operate "At Their Best." Thus, the healthy, high-performance pyramid brings us full cycle to what we wrote about in Chapter 2: Cultural transformation requires, and starts with, personal transformation.

Questions to Consider

1. Does your organization or group have a clear and compelling vision? If not, what do you think it should be? What is your purpose?

   _____

   _____

   _____

2. How well do people understand the connection between culture and strategy?

   _____

   _____

   _____

3. What value is most needed to drive your organization's strategy?

   _____

   _____

   _____

FINAL THOUGHTS ON LEADERSHIP, TEAMS AND CULTURE

Culture *does* matter. The health of your team matters. Your organization, group or team has a culture; your only choice is whether to let it shape you, or to influence it.

It helps to know what aspects of your culture you want to shift and how that will make a difference. Various situations place a premium on specific cultural values:

- Cross-organizational collaboration—when turf issues are common

- Empowered employees—when hierarchy prevails

- High personal accountability—when people are feeling victimized, not accountable

- Openness to change—when resistance is prevalent

- Innovation and risk-taking—when old-school thinking creates risk-aversion

- Wiser thinking and perspective—when people are hectic and frantic

- A focus on organizational health—when people are overly stressed and burned out

Results are diminished by unhealthy cultures, and there is also a human price that is paid as a result of the ineffective implementation of change. This takes the form of:

- Disenfranchised employees

- Loss of loyalty, trust and commitment

- High levels of stress and burnout

- Poor balance in life and neglected families

The answer to superior competitive performance and more fulfillment for people can be found in the qualities of a healthy culture and an enlightened 21st century style of leadership.

WHAT A SUCCESSFUL ORGANIZATION LOOKS LIKE IN CULTURAL TERMS

- Managers more like coaches, less like supervisors or bosses
- More influence and facilitation skills, less command-and-control
- Rewards for adding value, not based on position, title or longevity
- Continuous education to match the changing environment
- Managers promoted for their ability to learn and train others
- Fewer checks, audits and control steps
- Flatter, less hierarchical organizational structure
- Fewer functional departments, more process teams
- Team-oriented incentives replace individual recognition

Figure 17.1 © 2006 Senn-Delaney Leadership Consulting Group, LLC.

A Model for 21st Century Leadership

"Just as we need more people to provide leadership in the complex organizations that dominate our world today, we also need more people to develop the cultures that will create that leadership."

John Kotter[43]

You may be reading this and asking yourself the question, "What can I do if I'm not the CEO and we are not actively addressing culture?" You can make a difference even if you are not the top leader, or if your organization is not addressing its culture. Everyone influences the culture around them, in their organization, their department or their own work team. Each of us casts a shadow by our own behaviors, and each of us has a choice in terms of our own personal and professional development.

Remember, organizational transformation does not take place without personal transformation. If everyone waits for those above them or around them to change, no one changes. This is the time when each of us needs to look at ourselves and decide how we can change in order to better live the Essential Values and be "at our best."

The chart below shows some of the transitions Senn-Delaney Leadership believes individuals need to make to better contribute to healthy cultures and business results:

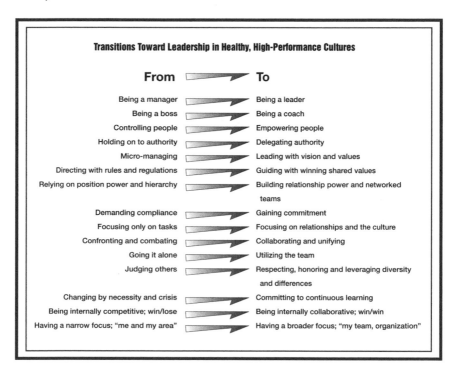

Transitions Toward Leadership in Healthy, High-Performance Cultures

From	To
Being a manager	Being a leader
Being a boss	Being a coach
Controlling people	Empowering people
Holding on to authority	Delegating authority
Micro-managing	Leading with vision and values
Directing with rules and regulations	Guiding with winning shared values
Relying on position power and hierarchy	Building relationship power and networked teams
Demanding compliance	Gaining commitment
Focusing only on tasks	Focusing on relationships and the culture
Confronting and combating	Collaborating and unifying
Going it alone	Utilizing the team
Judging others	Respecting, honoring and leveraging diversity and differences
Changing by necessity and crisis	Committing to continuous learning
Being internally competitive; win/lose	Being internally collaborative; win/win
Having a narrow focus; "me and my area"	Having a broader focus; "my team, organization"

Figure 17.2 © 2006 Senn-Delaney Leadership Consulting Group, LLC.

Final Thoughts on Culture

All that you do or attempt to do in your organization will be impacted by your culture. Therefore, you might want to keep these points in mind:

- Your organization has a culture, whether you want it to or not.

- The only choice you have is whether you proactively influence it or not.

- Whether you lead a company, department or team, you influence the culture of that group by the shadow you cast. Who you are and how you behave speaks louder than any words you choose to use.

- A healthy, high-performance culture is the greatest asset an organization or team can have.

- Even though these are hectic times, you can operate without undue stress if your organization has a healthy culture and you maintain a healthy state of mind.

For those organizations and individuals working on culture shaping, we make the following recommendations:

- Be as committed to culture shaping as you are to achieving your objective goals.

- Utilize systematic change-management processes and training to address leadership skills, teambuilding and culture shaping.

- If you are involved in acquisitions or mergers, beware of cultural clash. Pay as much attention to the cultural integration as you do to business integration.

- Engage in culture shaping concurrently with business change initiatives to maximize efficiency and provide synergy. They support one another.

- Counsel your resistors, in or out—especially those among senior management. There is no room for spectators in the process of culture shaping.

- Communicate—appreciate—communicate.

- Celebrate the little wins along the way.

- Laugh a lot; laughter is therapeutic for everyone!

FINAL THOUGHTS ON LIVING LIFE AT YOUR BEST

In this age of rapid change, teams come and go, as do jobs. Therefore the most important take-away for you may be the ideas we've shared on *living life at your best*. Check your Mood Elevator often and know that you can live more of your life on the higher floors. Also know that everyone visits the lower floors on occasion. When you find yourself there, trust that it will pass, as it is not your natural state. And, in the meantime, do as little damage to yourself and others as you can.

Pay attention to all aspects of your own health—physical, mental and spiritual. Watch your energy level and your state of mind. Be accountable for the shadow cast by your words, deeds and moods. Above all, maintain your perspective. We all face challenges, but we all have so much to be grateful for compared to so many others in the world. Remember that gratitude is the express button on the Mood Elevator and your mood determines your effectiveness as well as your quality of life.

Finally, remember that life, like culture shaping, is a journey—not a destination. Each of us is "a work in progress." Make sure you enjoy that journey along the way!

ABOUT SENN-DELANEY LEADERSHIP

Senn-Delaney Leadership is the oldest, most experienced and most successful culture-shaping firm in the world. Their leadership, teambuilding and culture-shaping process has been used by hundreds of organizations including Fortune 500 and Global 1000 CEO's, governors of states, members of a U.S. President's cabinet, city governments in Europe and deans of graduate schools of business and their faculty.

Our Mission

Their mission for the past 28 years has been to: create healthy, high-performance organizational cultures, to consistently achieve better business results.

The most common reasons they are asked to work with organizations are to:

- Quickly align new CEO's and their senior teams

- Avoid cultural clash in mergers and acquisitions

- Reduce silos and turf and create shared organizational model

- Create winning cultures to support new strategies

- Create service cultures or support Six Sigma and lean manufacturing

- Build bench strength with customized CEO-led leadership development programs

Senn-Delaney Leadership has measurably shifted behaviors of hundreds of organizations, thousands of teams, tens of thousands of leaders and hundreds of thousands of their employees. They accomplish this by using the comprehensive, time-tested change process described in this book. The process is customized to the needs and goals of clients and includes:

- Insightful diagnostics

- Customized team seminars

- A train-the-client-facilitator transfer of competence process

- One-on-one coaching of CEO's and senior executives

- An individual and team reinforcement process including the eCoach®

- Alignment of all client internal reinforcement systems

- Measurement of results for individuals, teams and organizations

All of Senn-Delaney Leadership's partners and consultants have decades of hands-on business experience as line executives, plus years of training in the Senn-Delaney processes. The Senn-Delaney team works together with its clients' top leaders and internal change agents in a custom-tailored process. They normally start with the CEO and the senior team and facilitate the process throughout the organization.

Senn-Delaney Leadership's proven process:

- Creates winning cultures

- Helps teams align and make decisions faster

- Increases organization-wide teamwork to support cross-organizational initiatives

- Creates a culture that better supports strategies

- Builds bench strength

- Brings values to life

- Increases innovation, agility and openness to change

Senn-Delaney Leadership is an international firm of leadership consultants who are passionate about making a difference in organizations. They serve their clients worldwide through offices in California, New York and London.

You can learn more about the firm on their website: www.senndelaney.com

You may contact the corporate headquarters for more information about the services of Senn-Delaney Leadership, or to obtain copies of this book or other books co-authored by Larry Senn, including:

- Leaders on Leading: Insights from the Field

- The Team at the Top—Is It Really a Team?

- Cultural Clash in Mergers and Acquisitions

Corporate Headquarters:
Senn-Delaney Leadership Consulting Group, LLC.
3780 Kilroy Airport Way, Suite 800
Long Beach, CA 90806
Main Phone (562) 426-5400
Fax (562) 426-5174
Business Development (562) 981-5211
info@senndelaney.com

ACKNOWLEDGEMENTS TO THE CONTRIBUTORS TO THE BOOK

THE CEO's WHO MADE THIS POSSIBLE

We started the book by saying it was "a view from the field" based on experiences over the years with client organizations. We thank the countless internal change agents and client facilitators we have partnered with. Most of all we are indebted to the CEO's who sponsored and led the culture-shaping processes. While there are too many to mention, we want to acknowledge the organizations and their leaders that appear in stories and examples in the book. They include, in alphabetical order:

- Jim Albaugh, President and CEO, Boeing IDS

- Doug Briggs, former CEO, QVC, Inc.

- Craven Crowell, former Chairman, Tennessee Valley Authority (TVA)

- Peter Darbee, President and CEO, PG&E

- Bill Davila former President, The Vons Companies, Inc.

- Robert Dotson, President and CEO, T-Mobile USA , Inc.

- Bill Ferguson, former CEO, NYNEX

- Neil Fiske, CEO, Bath and Body Works

- Mary Foster, former President, Sylvan Learning Centers

- Mark Frissora, former Chairman, President and CEO, Tenneco

- Larry Glasscock, Chairman, President and CEO, WellPoint, Inc.

- Joe Hudson former Chairman, J.L. Hudson Company

- Jerry Jurgensen, Chairman and CEO, Nationwide

- Al Landon, Chairman, President and CEO, Bank of Hawaii

- Glenn McCullough, Chairman, Tennessee Valley Authority (TVA)

- Henry Meyer, Chairman, President and CEO, KeyCorp

- Mike O'Neil, former CEO, Bank of Hawaii

- David Novak, Chairman, President and CEO, Yum! Brands, Inc.

- Ivan Seidenberg, Chairman and CEO, Verizon

- Ray Smith, former CEO, Bell Atlantic

- Ken Stevens, CFO, Limited Brands, Inc.

- Phil Swash, VP of Operations, Airbus

- Jack Welch, former Chairman, General Electric

The Senn-Delaney Team

Like the team-based firm we run, this book has been the work of many people. In more ways than can be described. The team of office staff at Senn-Delaney Leadership have supported our writing, challenged and built upon our ideas, created customized graphics, read through countless drafts, and offered significant suggestions.

We want to specifically thank the following people who contributed their time to this project: The overall project manager was our Communications Director Celeste Rothstein. The look of the book its layout and the cover were created by our Graphic Designer Paul Diniakos. Other contributors from our Product Development Group included Peter Brown who created many of the original figures in the book and Darin Senn for his work with Peter to create the DURAM™ graphic model. Typing and proofing fell largely to Judy Gesicki, Executive Assistant to Larry Senn and Jim Hart and Margee Infante, Resource Manager at Senn-Delaney Leadership.

Our Outside Partners

We thank Ken Shelton and his team at Leadership Excellence for their help in editing the first draft and Contributing Editor, Susanne R. Stoeckeler for her work on the final edits.

Finally, we wish to thank Dr. William B. Wolf, former professor at USC, for starting Senn-Delaney Leadership on this journey by encouraging Larry to enroll in the doctoral program in 1962 and sponsoring his doctoral dissertation on corporate culture.

SOURCES

Introduction

1. Larry E. Senn, *Organizational Character as a Tool in the Analysis of Business Organizations*, unpublished doctoral dissertation, University of Southern California, Los Angeles, 1970

2. Thomas J. Peters and Robert H. Waterman, *In Search of Excellence*; New York: Harper & Row, 1982

3. Larry E. Senn and John R. Childress, *The Secret of a Winning Culture*; Los Angeles: The Leadership Press, 1999

Chapter 1

4. "Corporate Culture: The Hard-to-Change Values that Spell Success or Failure," *Business Week*, October 27, 1980, pp. 148-160

5. Nitin Nohria and James D. Berkley, "Whatever Happened to the Take-Charge Manager?", *Harvard Business Review*, January-February 1994, pp. 128-137

6. "Corporate Culture: The Hard-to-Change Values that Spell Success or Failure" pp. 148-160

7. Mitchell Lee Marks and Philip Harold Mirvis, "The Merger Syndrome," *Psychology Today*, October 1986

8. Beverly Geber, "The Forgotten Factor in Merger Mania," *Training Magazine*, February 1987

9. K. Cahill, "Bridging the culture gap," *CFO: The Magazine for Senior Financial Executives*, v12n4, Apr 1996, p.15

10.Dan Ciampa, "Almost Ready: How Leaders Move Up," *Harvard Business Review*, January 2005, Vol. 83, p. 46

11.Welch, Jack, Chairman and Chief Executive Officer, General Electric. Personal interview, 1993. For the book, *21st Century Leadership—Dialogues with 100 Top Leaders*, Los Angeles: The Leadership Press, 1993

12.Lynn Joy McFarland, Larry E. Senn, and John R. Childress, *21st Century Leadership: Dialogues with 100 Top Leaders*, p. 130

13.As quoted by Bruce Caldwell, "Missteps, Miscues," *Information Week*, June 20, 1994

14.Larry E. Senn and John R. Childress, *In the Eye of the Storm;* Los Angeles: The Leadership Press, 1995, p. 38

15.Kristen Hays, "Enron Schemes Reflect Culture, Report's Author Says," *Los Angeles Times*, Feb 10, 2003, page C3

CHAPTER 2

16.Daniel Goleman, *Emotional Intelligence: Why It Can Matter More than IQ*, New York: Bantam, 1995

17.Daniel Goleman, *Primal Leadership: Realizing the Power of Emotional Intelligence*, Boston: Harvard Business School Press, 2002

18.C.W. Metcalf, *Humor, Risk and Change*™ (video recording) produced by American Media, Inc., Des Moines, Iowa, 1990

CHAPTER 3

19.As quoted by Larry E. Senn and John R. Childress, *The Secret of a Winning Culture*, Los Angeles: Leadership Press, 1999, p. 82.

20.*21st Century Leadership: Dialogues with 100 Top Leaders*, page 151

21. *21st Century Leadership: Dialogues with 100 Top Leaders*, page 125

CHAPTER 4

22. Elizabeth G. Chambers, Mark Foulon, Helen Handfield-Jones, Steven M. Hankin, Edward G. Michaels III, "The War for Talent," *The McKinsey Quarterly*, 1998 Number 3

CHAPTER 5

23. "Tennessee Valley Authority Principles,"www.tva.gov/foia/readroom/policy/prinprac/tvastrat.htm, September 2001

24. Ken Blanchard, Jim Ballard, Fred Finch, *Customer Mania!: It's Never Too Late to Build a Customer-Focused Company*, New York: Free Press, a division of Simon and Schuster, 2004, pp. 14-22

CHAPTER 7

25. Schein, Edgar, *How Culture Forms, Develops and Changes*, Jossey-Bass, 1985, p.19

26. "The World's Most Admired Companies," *Fortune*, March 7, 2005

27. Smith, Ray, Chairman and Chief Executive Officer, Bell Atlantic Corporation. Personal interview with Larry Senn, 1992.

28. W. Brooke Tunstall, *Disconnecting Parties: Managing the Bell System Break-Up, an Inside View*, New York: McGraw-Hill, 1985

29. Bell Atlantic Corporation, 1992. Used with permission.

Chapter 8

30 John P. Kotter and James L. Heskett, *Corporate Culture and Performance*, New York: Free Press, a division of Simon and Schuster, 1992

31. *In the Eye of the Storm*, p.121

32. Charles J. Sykes, *A Nation of Victims*, New York: St. Martin's Press, 1992, p. 13, 253

33. Jon R. Katzenbach and Douglas K. Smith, *The Wisdom of Teams*, (Massachusetts: Harvard Business School Press, 1993), p. 15

34. *The Secret of a Winning Culture*, p. 22

Chapter 9

35. This graphic was used in the book, *The Forgotten Half of Change; Achieving Greater Creativity Though Changes in Perception* (Chicago: Dearborn Trade Press, 2005). The author, Luc de Brabandere, was unable to locate the original source, and after a good deal of research, we were similarly unsuccessful. If you have any information regarding the artist or source of this image, please contact Senn-Delaney Leadership.

Chapter 12

36. "E-mails 'Hurt IQ More than Pot'," CNN.com, April 22, 2005 (http://edition.cnn.com/2005/WORLD/europe/04/22/text.iq/index.html)

Chapter 14

37. Jeffrey McCracken, "'Way Forward' Requires Culture Shift at Ford," *The Wall Street Journal*, January 23, 2006

38. *The Secret of a Winning Culture*, p. 147

39. *The Secret of a Winning Culture*, p. 22

40. Diane Brady, "The Immelt Revolution," *Business Week*, March 28,2005, p. 64

41. Personal correspondence from Doug Briggs to Larry Senn dated July 1, 1996

CHAPTER 16

42. *21st Century Leadership: Dialogues with 100 Top Leaders*, p. 99

CHAPTER 17

43. John P. Kotter, *John P. Kotter on What Leaders Really Do*, (Boston: Harvard Business School Press, 1999), p. 65

INDEX

C

F

M

P

Q

R

T

W

Y

Z